COURTS
&
HUNGER

COURTS & HUNGER

Sanjay Parikh

Vani Book Company
(An Imprint of Vani Prakashan Group)

Vani Book Company
(An Imprint of Vani Prakashan Group)
Head Office

4695, 21-A, Daryaganj, New Delhi 110 002, India
Phone +91 11 23273167 Fax : +91 11 23275710

Registered Bookstores and Offices

Ashok Rajpath, Patna 800 004, Bihar
Coffee House Campus, Mahatma Gandhi Marg, Allahabad 211 001, Uttar Pradesh
Mahatma Gandhi International Hindi University, Wardha 442 001, Maharashtra
Sultania Road, Motia Park , Bhopal 462 001, Madhya Pradesh
Goripur Taliya Para, 313, R.B.C. Road 24- Parganas (North) Kolkata 743 166, West Bengal

www.vaniprakashan.com
marketing@vaniprakashan.in
sales@vaniprakashan.in

Courts & Hunger
by Sanjay Parikh

ISBN : 978-93-5518-114-5
Non-Fiction/Law/Social Science

First Edition 2022

Price : ₹ 699

Printed and bound in India at Thomson Press (India) Ltd.

Vani Prakashan's signature motif is created by Artist Maqbool Fida Husain

To my Parents

Maa and Babuji
Who had answers to many
questions which I now seek alone

Foreword

Courts and Hunger is a moving account of how nature's frown and insensitiveness of man can make life of a large segment of the population remain untouched by the blessings of democracy and the benign touch of a welfare state. Illiteracy, ignorance and poverty are curses on the poor. This was the story of the people of Kalahandi, Balangir and Koraput (KBK) districts in Odisha. Thanks to the benign intervention of the Supreme Court of India much ameliorative change has occurred.

Sri Sanjay Parikh is a senior lawyer with a rare sensitivity towards human suffering. His record as a defender of public interest and human rights is most impressive. A considerable part of his professional time and services is devoted to public-interest. He has presented many meticulously prepared social issues before the courts. His heart beats for the poor and the under-privileged. Of such men, it is admiringly said, that they have grown two-blades of grass where one grew and deserve the better of mankind.

In this book he narrates the history of the reformative action initiated in the 'KBK' districts by the Supreme Court of India with the assistance of the National Human Rights Commission of India and his own significant role. He provides an informative survey of the concept of the 'Right to Food' as propounded by the Supreme Court of India and its implications on the duties of the State. This concept has been the subject matter of serious international discourse. Sri Parikh takes us through the evolution of this idea in international understanding and draws attention to the creative role of the Supreme Court.

The author refers to the long and tortuous history of this area:

> Mahatma Gandhi had visited Puri in March, 1921 and was shocked to see "the crowd of men, women and children with their fleshless ribs". He later

wrote in Harijan, "Orissa is the epitome of India's poverty". What Gandhiji said then is true even today. While the other places in Odisha have seen some improvement over time, the situation in KBK largely remains the same. Any reference to Kalahandi, Balangir and Koraput (KBK, in short) immediately evokes the grim picture of emaciated human figures, poverty, suffering and death. What are the reasons for such suffering? Are the natural calamities, like drought, the cause of it or is it on account of continued human apathy and neglect.

Out of Odisha's 30 districts, Kalahandi, Balangir and Koraput situated in southern and western Odisha, are the most backward regions. Since 1992-93, KBK districts have been further subdivided into 8 districts. These 8 districts contain 19.72% of the population and span more than 30.59% of the geographical area of the state. Majority of the population of KBK still lives in villages and belongs largely to Scheduled Castes and Tribes. These districts suffer from chronic malnutrition, food scarcity, and migration resulting from failure to produce sufficient crops, lack of availability of services and entitlements.

The sordid story of human suffering had its origin in the insensitivity of the administration. At the bottom of it all is the idea that developmental issues are based on the idea of 'Welfare' and on the basis of 'Rights'.

Hernando de Soto in his *The Mystery of Capital* sends out the stirring message that the source of prosperity is not foreign aid, but lies in our own unexplored backyard.

> By our calculations, [de Soto and his team] the total value of the real estate held but not legally owned by the poor of the Third World and former communist nations is at least $ 9.3 trillion".
>
> This is a number worth pondering. $ 9.3 trillion is about twice as much as the total circulating U.S. money supply....It is more than twenty times the total direct foreign investment into all Third World and former communist countries in the ten years after 1989, forty-six times the World Bank loans of the past three decades, and ninety-three times as much as all the development assistance from all advanced countries to the Third World in the same period.

Despite India's great cultural and civilisational legacy, inequalities of Indian society are appalling. There is economic and social anaemia at one extreme end and apoplexy at the other. It is truly said that unequal societies live under a constant dread of an impending disaster. The contribution of the poor in nation building is enormous. They have helped build projects at places even difficult to access. They are not the problem but quite often, they are the solution.

In this sensitive work the author brings out vividly the harrowing story of administrative apathy and how judicial interventions become crucial. Sri Sanjay's disenchantment that 'We can, by our efforts, try to bridge the gap but the ideal equality remains an utopia' is an embarrassing reality.

—M.N. Venkatachaliah

Introduction

WHAT PROMPTED me to write this book, when in this day and age, anyone can—as in the case of any other legal matter—easily access the net to research or investigate what transpired in the proceedings before the Supreme Court as well as the National Human Rights Commission (NHRC) relating to the starvation death cases occurring in the Kalahandi, Balangir and Koraput (KBK) districts of Odisha?* The reason, I think, for me, they were not mere proceedings. They were deeply connected with some questions that had arisen decades back when I was a child, somewhere in the early seventies.

At that time, my father was posted at Agra. We were living in a railway quarter. One day, around eight in the morning, when I came out of my house, I saw a girl with a frail frame wearing a shabby frock. She was looking quite miserable. She must have been around 7-8 years old. I saw her picking up something from the grass and consuming it. I was keen to know what exactly she was eating. I went near her. I found, to my utter shock, that she was picking up particles of rice thrown out as waste by a family in our neighbourhood. The incident left a deep impact on me. It is still vivid in my memory.

I could not, however, logically connect all the different factors which could answer my curiosity—why on earth was this girl so hungry that, like an animal, she was eating discarded food particles from the grass? I came back home and told my mother what I had seen. She immediately gave me a *roti*. I came out to give it to her but could not find her. She left me with a pang. Something troubled me for days except that my

* KBK now includes 8 districts: Kalahandi, Balangir, Koraput, Malkangiri, Nabarangpur, Rayagada, Subarnapur and Nuapada.

questioning did not take me on the path of Buddha! Later, during my college days, in a magazine, I saw a frail, skeleton-like figure of a tribal from Kalahandi. The article was on drought and famine recurring in this part of Odisha (then Orissa). The picture reminded me of the girl. I wondered if it would ever be possible to cure hunger, to ensure that nobody died due to lack of food?

Years passed. I completed my law degree and came to Delhi. I joined Justice S. Rangarajan* in 1982 as an advocate in the Supreme Court. Within a few months, we developed a warm relationship. As a result, I could, without hesitation, ask him questions on different aspects of life, knowing that even if my questions were stupid, he would not ridicule me. Besides philosophy and law, his knowledge of economics was quite profound.

One afternoon, I found him free and in a good mood. I decided to ask him the question that had been troubling me all these years: how can we call ourselves selfless and not feel guilty when someone outside has no food to eat whereas we have ample? After hearing my question, he asked me to reformulate it several times. I did so. Then he asked me to write it down. I did that with some explanations attached. He told me about the Upanishads, the theory of karma, Marx's understanding of inequality, Rawls' treatise on a pragmatic concept of equality, etc. The sum and substance of what he said was that inequality as a harsh reality exists in the world. We can, by our efforts, try to bridge the gap but ideal equality will remain an utopia. I was not satisfied but I probably could not question him further as the discussion entered into subtle areas of right and wrong, ideals and morals, existential truth, dharma and so on, the synthesis of which was not possible. It ended there.

It so happened that after a few years, I met Kishen Pattanayak*, who had come to Delhi to file a petition in connection with the persistent

---

* Justice S. Rangarajan was a Judge of the Delhi High Court, from 1969 to 1976, when he was transferred to the Gauhati High Court as a measure of punishment for quashing the detention of Kuldip Nayar, a veteran journalist, during the Emergency. He was re-transferred to the Delhi High Court in 1977 and thereafter, appointed as Chairman of the Monopolies and Restrictive Trade Practices Commission, from where he retired in September 1981. After retirement, he practiced at the Supreme Court as a Senior Advocate.

problem of starvation deaths in Kalahandi. He wanted to argue it in person. Immediately, the childhood memory of the starving girl appeared once again before my eyes. Curious, I asked him about the causes of poverty and starvation deaths. He explained the problem in a simple way. I could not, however, draw a connection between the government's inaction and a recurring natural calamity.

Pattanayak argued his petition in person in the Supreme Court and a judgment came in 1989, containing promises by the Odisha government to improve the situation in KBK. However, the situation did not improve; promises remained on paper; hunger and starvation deaths continued.

In the judgment, the Court had given Pattanayak liberty to come back, if further directions were needed. When I met him again, he looked disheartened and said that it would not be possible for him to start the battle all over again. I expressed my wish to take it forward, to see it to its logical end. He was quite happy and showed his willingness to provide guidance, when required. I persuaded the Indian Council of Legal Aid and Advice to take up this great cause. The Council agreed. PUCL and others also joined. Dr. Amrita Rangasamy*, who was already working on poverty issues, also joined the petition.

The Writ Petition, which was initially filed in the Supreme Court, was sent to the NHRC for identifying the causes of starvation and to come up with a permanent solution. I was initially disappointed when the Supreme Court itself did not take up this important issue, but discovered later that it was a godsent opportunity.

Justice M.N. Venkatachaliah, former Chief Justice of India, was the Chairperson of NHRC at that time. The first hearing was quite formal. But during the second hearing, Justice Venkatachaliah, after fully comprehending the problem, told the parties that the Commission would take up the matter as non-contentious and would proceed with the full cooperation of all the parties. Then he looked at me and said: "Sanjay, you prepare the parameters of different issues and suggest ways to solve the problem. Feel as if you are the Planning Commission for this purpose!" This was an extraordinary gesture. For a moment I became speechless.

---

* Social activist and former Member of Parliament from Odisha.

I had no scheme in my mind but was overwhelmed by the confidence reposed in me. I prepared a scheme after reading the available material and discussing it with my friends and experts. The scheme—containing short-term and long-term action plans—was handed over to the Commission. The Commission adopted an innovative method for approaching the issue. It asked the Centre and the State of Odisha to provide it with their annual targets for all their social schemes. These were then divided into quarterly targets. The methodology was that the state would submit quarterly targets, which would be physically verified by a Special Rapporteur. On the report of the Special Rapporteur, suggestions from the parties would be taken and after recording satisfaction or otherwise, the Commission would proceed further for the next quarterly target.

This process continued for over a decade. The foundation was laid down during the tenure of Justice Venkatachaliah. But the proceedings were continued in the same spirit by his successors: Justice J.S. Verma and Justice A.S. Anand—both, former Chief Justices of India. The directions and the proceedings of the NHRC were finally accepted by the Supreme Court by its order dated 22.1.2008.

How did the proceedings take shape? How did clarity on issues emerge? How did gradual transformation come to KBK? What was the net result? An attempt has been made to answer these questions in this book.

It came out clearly from this elaborate exercise that the reasons for starvation deaths were not droughts. It was a man-made disaster and State's insensitive approach was responsible for people's sufferings.

Eventually, a significant change was brought on the ground as well as in the mindset of the authorities in grappling with the problems of the KBK districts. But it required a consistent and sincere effort by the government to continue from the point where the Supreme Court and the NHRC left off. The state has a duty to see that the next generation does not face the brunt of decades of wrongs, hunger, under-nutrition, malnutrition and starvation deaths. Unfortunately, it appears from subsequent developments, that the state did not pursue the activity with

---

* Director, Centre for the Studies of Administration of Relief, New Delhi.

the same enthusiasm. However, the myth of drought being the cause of starvation deaths was exposed. No longer could the state be heard to blame nature for its own inaction and negligence. I learnt a lot from this case. It gave me a sense of self-fulfilment. In a limited sense, it allowed me an opportunity to purge myself of the guilt which I had developed as a child. The questions, however, are still not answered.

I tried to narrate the NHRC proceedings in a simple way but found that I could not avoid the details as they represent the process of giving actual shape to the 'entitlement approach'. They show how a human rights mechanism can help in addressing the problem of hunger caused due to a state's inactions and how systematic monitoring can bring a change. I have given appropriate headings to the proceedings to make them a bit more interesting.

I must whole-heartedly appreciate the commendable work done by Shri Chaman Lal, the Special Rapporteur. He carried, with his visits to the KBK, a true picture of the situation on the ground, with lots of factual data. His inputs helped the NHRC in making appropriate recommendations.

I ought to have brought this book out much earlier but due to the demands of my professional involvements, the continuity broke several times. At some stage, a doubt also arose about whether this effort was worthwhile after a long gap? My friends and associates, however, encouraged me with this endeavour and I was also convinced that the problems discussed here are very much relevant and alive, not only for the KBK, but for other states in the country as well. It applies not only in resolving several social and human rights' issues but also in situations where executive fails to deliver–whether during migration crises or in preventing deaths during Covid pandemic.

How much inequality, we as human beings, have created and how much of it we blame on God, are matters for introspection and self-realization. For my part, I can only hope that I will not see a child again having to pick up strains of rice fallen on the grass!

–Sanjay Parikh

Acknowledgements

I owe my sincere thanks to all who helped me in writing this book. When the case was pending before the NHRC, various inputs and suggestions were required. The replies of the State of Odisha and responses of the Special Rapporteur needed thorough analysis. Initially, my colleague Abhinash Kumar Mishra, Advocate was helping me. Later Advocate Shanmuga Patro came forward to help me. He hails from Odisha and was, therefore, aware of the ground realities of KBK. His inputs were very useful. Dr. Manoj Kumar Sinha (now Director - Indian Law Institute) graciously assisted me in compiling and analyzing the data with precision and also enriching my knowledge on the subject. After the case was over, the inner compulsion of writing about this worthwhile experience of nearly a decade, persisted. Lot of time was spent in arranging the papers which were occupying a sizable space in my office. Then the process of writing started, which continued in parts with long breaks.

In this process, the suggestions, research and help hich I received from Piyush Mohapatra, Ninni Susan Thomas, Moulshree Pathak and others is highly appreciable. Sanjana Srikumar, Advocate joined my office when the chapters were in loose form. She worked very hard to go through the material and making useful additions with foot-notes. I thank her profusely.

Dr. Claude Alvares, Founder–Goa Foundation (NGO) is not only a family friend and a well-wisher but a source of inspiration. When I gave him the draft copy for corrections, he accepted it happily and ensured that the book is free from any mistakes.

I am also very thankful to Arun Maheshwariji and Aditi of Vani Prakashan, who readily accepted my request to publish this book. My son Satwik did final cross-checking and reading. My deep appreciation for his efforts. My apologies if I have failed to acknowledge anyone.

I have no words to express my gratitude to Justice M.N. Venkatachaliah, whom I respect and adore, not only because of his deep knowledge and simplicity but for having innate qualities of a great human being. He agreed, without a moment's hesitation, to write the preface of this book. My salutations!

Contents

Profiles of KBK Districts

Mahatma Gandhi had visited Puri in March, 1921 and was shocked to see "the crowd of men, women and children with their fleshless ribs".[1] He later wrote in *Harijan*, "Orissa is the epitome of India's poverty".[2] What Gandhiji said then is true even today. While the other places in Odisha have seen some improvement over time, the situation in KBK largely remains the same. Any reference to Kalahandi, Balangir and Koraput (KBK, in short) immediately evokes the grim picture of emaciated human figures, poverty, suffering and death. What are the reasons for such suffering? Are the natural calamities, like drought, the cause of it or is it on account of continued human apathy and neglect? Before seeking answers to these questions, one must know something, in howsoever brief a manner, about the place and its inhabitants.

The history of Odisha is quite ancient. Several royal dynasties ruled the region, which was also known as Kaushala, Kalinga (ruled by emperor Ashoka), Odra and Utkal with some changes in its boundaries over time.[3] Odisha represented a great culture and was a place known for art, artefacts, music and dance. The region was invaded by Afghans in 1568. The domination of the Afghans continued for some time, followed by a series of battles between Afghans and Mughals. The Mughals were finally successful in establishing their control in 1593 which they retained for a considerable period. After the decline of the Mughals, the Nawabs of Bengal and even the Marathas were among its rulers. Orissa came under British rule from 1803 to 1947.

Bihar and Orissa Province was separated from Bengal Presidency in 1912. Orissa (present-day Odisha) became an independent province on April, 1, 1936. The day is celebrated annually as *Utkal Divas*, in memory of the state's formation and recognition of its distinct linguistic identity. In 1956, the President of India declared 62 communities of Odisha as

Scheduled Tribes. Out of them, 13 are Primitive Tribal Groups (PTGs). Out of the total land area of Odisha, 44.25% is Scheduled Area, and 22% of the total population of the state are Scheduled Tribes.[4] The major tribes include the Gond, Kondh, Santhal, Saora, Bhuiyan, Paraja, Koya, Oraon, Gadaba, Juanga and the Munda. There are several other smaller tribal groups as well. These tribes survive mainly on land and forest resources, including minor forest produce.

Out of Odisha's 30 districts, Kalahandi, Balangir and Koraput, situated in southern and western Odisha, are the most backward regions. Since 1992-93, KBK districts have been further subdivided into 8 districts.[5] These 8 districts contain 19.72% of the population and span more than 30.59% of the geographical area of the state. Majority of the population of KBK still lives in villages and belongs largely to Scheduled Castes and Tribes. These districts suffer from chronic malnutrition, food scarcity, and migration resulting from failure to produce sufficient crops, lack of availability of services and entitlements.[6] The region has always been prone to natural calamities, which further add to the misery of the population mainly owing to its high dependence on agriculture.

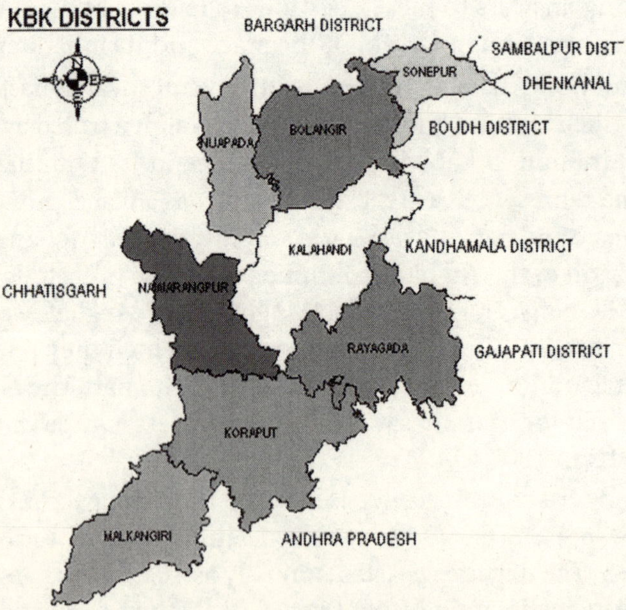

Map of KBK districts[7]

Surprisingly, these districts experience such severe malnutrition despite their abundant natural resources and water systems. The tributaries of the Mahanadi and the Godavari, though primarily rain-fed, run through them. The area has seven types of soils, suitable for the cultivation of most crops, as well as tracts of dense forests.

However, deforestation and soil erosion have led to deep ecological imbalances in the area, naturally aggravating poverty and hunger. Droughts had occurred in Kalahandi in 1868, 1884 and 1897 and a severe famine was witnessed in 1899. In 1919-20 another drought occurred and it was followed by diseases like cholera, influenza and malnutrition due to scarcity of food. Thereafter, a series of droughts took place in the region during 1922-1923, 1925-1926, 1929-1930 1954-1955, 1955-56, 1965-66, 1974-75 and also in 1985. These recurring calamities were accompanied by failures of successive governments to mitigate their effects, without any long-term efforts to ameliorate the situation.

The demographics of the districts and their forest cover are summarized in the following table:

District Profile (as per 2011 census)[8]

District	Total Population as of 2011	Percentage of SC Population	Percentage of ST	Sex Ratio	Forest Cover
Koraput	1,3,79,647	14.25%	50.56%	1032	21.89%
Rayagada	9,67,911	14.41%	55.99%	1051	44.3%
Malkangiri	6,13,192	22.55%	57.83%	1020	40.08%
Nabarangpur	12,20,946	14.53%	55.79%	1019	21.26%
Kalahandi	15,76,869	18.17%	28.5%	1003	30.39%
Nuapada	6,10,382	13.46%	33.8%	1021	32.19%
Balangir	16,48,997	17.88%	21.05%	987	14.25%
Subarnapur	6,10,183	25.6%	9.37%	960	14.12%

Koraput[9]

Koraput is located in the tribal belt of southern Odisha. The region has been ruled by many dynasties since the third century BC including the Satavahans, Ikshvakus, Nalas, Ganga kings and kings of Suryavanshi. It became a part of Odisha on 1 April, 1936, when the latter became a separate state. Earlier it was a part of the Visakhapatnam district under the Madras presidency. On 1 October, 1992, it was further divided into four districts—Koraput, Nabarangpur, Rayagada and Malkangiri.

Koraput district has a geographical area of 8807 sq km, with 2 sub-divisions, 14 Tehsils, 14 Blocks, 240 Gram Panchayats and 2,028 villages. It has abundant forests and perennial water streams. Nearly 90% of the population depends on agriculture. The district produces coffee, cashew, cotton, tobacco, fruits and vegetables. The food crops produced are paddy, millet, maize and pulses. This fairly fertile land is home to Odisha's vast tribal population. Many aboriginal tribes such as the Bagata and the Bonda live in Koraput, which is also known for its diverse mineral deposits. Despite the region's ecological richness, in 2006, the Ministry of Panchayati Raj named Koraput one of the country's 250 most backward districts.[10]

Rayagada[11]

The Rayagada district was carved out of the erstwhile Koraput district on 2 October, 1992. The district derived its name from 'Raya' means rock and 'Gadda' means deep holes, referring to deep holes found in the rocks of the region. Several coins, rock inscriptions and literature indicate that the region was prominent through large parts of human history. The region was under the rule of the Rastrik Kings, Kharvela (said to be the only Aryan emperor of Odisha), the Ganga Vanshi and Suryavanshi Kings, the Bahamanis and briefly, the Nandapur kingdom. It was subsequently under a Tehsil of Vijayanagaram and the Jeypore Zamindari during British rule. *Raya* means rock and *gadda* means deep holes, referring to the deep holes found in the rocks of the region.

Rayagada has as many as 512 remote and inaccessible pockets. The district comprises 2 sub-divisions, 11 blocks, 182 GPs and 2,667 villages. The district also has the best sex ratio in the state, as noted in the 2011 Census.[12] The area is home to several tribal communities such as the Dongria Kandha, classified as a Particularly Vulnerable Tribal Group (PVTG), who live in the terrains of the Niyamgiri hills. Other tribal groups in the region include the Gonds, Sountis, etc. Over half the population of the area belong to Scheduled Tribes and over 10% belong to the Scheduled Castes.

Malkangiri[13]

Malkangiri was initially a taluk of Nabarangpur under undivided Koraput district. On 1 October, 1992, it was carved out of Koraput and turned into a separate district. It covers an area of 5,791 sq km, which has an abundance of lush greenery. The district has one sub-division, 7 blocks, 7 Tehsils, 111 GPs and 1045 villages. The eastern part of the district has plenty of plateaus and valleys. These areas are sparsely inhabited by primitive tribes, notably Bondas, Koyas, Porajas, Bhumiyas and Didayis.

Nabarangpur[14]

Nabarangpur district was also carved out from the district of Koraput on 1 October, 1992. The district has one sub-division, 10 Blocks, 10 Tehsils, 169 Gram Panchayats, 885 villages and it shares its boundary in the north with Raipur, and in the west with the Bastar districts of Chhattisgarh. The districts situated on the east side of Nabarangpur are Kalahandi and Rayagada and on the south, Koraput.

Nabarangpur covers an area of 5,294 sq km. It also has a vast area of 1,583.4 sq km covered by forests of sal and bamboo. The river Indravati forms the border between Nabarangpur and Koraput district. Indravati river shares its southern boundary with Koraput district and eastern boundary with Kalahandi and Rayagarh districts. The major tribes in the area are the Mirganis, Malis, Sundhi, Bhumias, Dombs, Paraja, Kondhas and Gadavas.

Balangir[15]

Balangir district is located in the western part of Odisha. It was formed on 1 November 1949 after the merger of many princely states. The district of Balangir has the Gandhamardan hill in the northwest border, and many streams run through this region. The name Balangir is believed to have been derived from Balaramgarh, a 16th century fort which was built in this place by Raja Balram Deo. The district spans an area of 6,575 sq km, with red, alluvial, black and mixed red soils, and a cultivable area of 3,45,650 hectares. The area comprises 3 Sub-Divisions, 14 Blocks, 14 Tehsils, 285 GPs and 1,783 villages. Some of the major tribes in Balangir district are the Gond, Khond and the Saora. Over 70% of the population are dependent on agriculture, primarily producing paddy, and also pulses, vegetables, spices, etc.

Subarnapur[16]

Subarnapur district, also known as Sonepur, was carved out of Balangir on 1 April, 1993. The district comprises 2 Sub-divisions, 6 Blocks, 6 Tehsils, 109 GPs. It is flanked on the north and the east by Sambalpur district, on the south and the south-east by Boudh district, and the west by Balangir district. Subarnapur is recognized for its rich cultural heritage, arts and crafts especially textile works, brass metal works and stone carvings.

The history of Subarnapur has seen several ruling dynasties including the Bhanjas, the Somavamsis, the Telgu-chodas, the Kalachuais, the Gangas and the Chouhans. In 1943, Maharaja Sudhansu Sekher Singh Deo, the last Chouhan ruler, established a Council of Ministers to begin the process of democratization, following which the kingdom was merged with Orissa in 1948.

Forests cover 415.78 sq km which amounts to 17.79% of the total geographical area of the district. The district has the lowest tribal population of all the eight former KBK districts. The major tribes are the Saora, Khond and Gond.

Kalahandi[17]

Records showing Kalahandi as a separate state have existed over a considerable period. They indicate that Kalahandi was previously known as Karond. According to Lieutenant Elliot, Deputy Commissioner, Raipur (1856), "This dependency is known only on the Nagpur side as Kharonde (Karond), the Oriya name being Kalahandi, and as there is no place or village corresponding to the former name it would appear to be a corruption of the latter, though it has been originally entered in the accounts." The name Kalahandi translates into 'black pot', which is thought to allude to the black cotton soil of the area. After India's independence, Kalahandi, a previously princely state, joined Odisha in 1948.

Kalahandi is located at the south-western part of Odisha, bordered in the north by the Balangir and Nuapada districts, south by the

Nabarangpur, Koraput and Rayagada districts, and east by the Rayagada, Kandhamal and Boudh districts. The district covers a total area of 7,920 sq. km, divided into 2 Sub-Divisions, 13 Blocks, 13 Tehsils, 310 GPs and 2249 revenue villages.

Kalahandi is inhabited by around 50 tribal groups at present, which comprise one-fourth of the total population of the district. Some of the major tribal groups – Bhottada, Gond, Khond Holva and Lodhas – compose two-third of the total tribal population. Most of them are forest-dwellers who also depend on shifting cultivation for their livelihood. Certain areas of Kalahandi like the Niyamgiri hills are rich in minerals like bauxite and are inhabited by the Dongria Kondh, a particularly vulnerable tribal group. They worship Niyam Raja, a god that they believe resides in the Niyamgiri hills.[18]

The district's economy is mainly based on agriculture. Rice, cotton and paddy are grown here. Among forest-based products, mahua, kendu-leaf, wood, timber and bamboo are common. Kalahandi district supplies a large amount of raw materials to paper mills in the neighbouring district of Rayagada.

Nuapada[19]

Nuapada district is located in the western part of Odisha. Spread over an area of 3407.5 sq km, the district extends in the north, west and south to Raipur district in Madhya Pradesh and in the east to Bargarh, Balangir and Kalahandi districts. Nuapada, which earlier was a part of Kalahandi district, was divided on 27 March, 1993, into two parts (Kalahandi and Nuapada) for administrative convenience.

Nuapada's topography contains plains and rugged hills which belong to the main line of the Eastern Ghat mountains. Dense forests in the region are classified into sal, teak and miscellaneous forests. Timber, especially sal, is a forest product that contributes well to the local economy. Other common trees are bija, asan and bandhan. Minor forest produce of this region includes kendu leaf, bamboo, broom-grass, mahua flower and seed, antia bark and sabai-grass. The area is also rich in mineral deposits of laterite, graphite and bauxite. Despite all this, as per the 2011 census, 78% of Nuapada's total population fell Below Poverty Line (BPL).

References

1. Government of India, 1999; Speech of Mahatma Gandhi, *Young India*, 06.04.1921
2. Bijoyini Mohanty Government of India, 1999; Speech of Mahatma Gandhi, *Young India*, 06.04.1921, Subas Chandra Hazary, ed. *Political Economy of India: Retrospects and Prospects*, (New Delhi: APH Publishing, 1997), 210
3. Prafulla Samantra, Asif Das, "Odisha: Poverty, Corporate Plunder and Resistance", *Counter Currents*, accessed September 14, 2020, https://www.countercurrents.org/das240710.htm
4. See "Socio-Culture of Lodhas Tribe in Odisha", *The Researchers*, https://theresearchers.asia/Papers/Vol-IV,%20Issue-I-2018/Socio-Culture%20of%20Lodhas%20Tribe%20in%20Odisha.pdf
5. These are Koraput, Malkangiri, Nabarangpur, Rayagada, Balangir, Subarnapur, Kalahandi and Nuapada. These eight districts comprise 14 sub-divisions, 80 tehsils, and as many Community Development Blocks.
6. Andaleeb Rahman, "Universal food security program and nutritional intake: Evidence from the hunger prone KBK districts in Odisha", Sciencedirect, *Food Policy* 63 (August 2016): 85, https://doi.org/10.1016/j.foodpol.2016.07.003
7. "KBK districts: A unique approach towards development" http://kbk.nic.in/pdf/KBKProfile.pdf
8. "District Wise Forest Cover of Odisha (as per 2013 Assessment)", ENVIS Centre of Odisha's State of Environment, accessed August 11, 2020, http://orienvis.nic.in/WriteReadData/links/District%20Wise%20Forest%20Cover%20of%20Odisha-711065821.doc

   District Census HandBook-Odisha, https://censusindia.gov.in/2011 census/dchb/Odisha.html, accessed August 11, 2020
9. Koraput, "About District", Govt. of Odisha, last modified Sep 10, 2020, https://koraput.nic.in/about-district/
10. See "Women Self Help Group Members Join Hands to Adopt Total Sanitation in Koraput District", https://jalshakti-ddws.gov.in/sites/default/files/Executive_summary_SHG_SLBMFO.pdf

    In fact, all 8 districts feature in the most backward 250 districts.
11. "About Rayagada", Govt. of Odisha, last modified Sep 09, 2020, https://rayagada.nic.in/about-district
12. "District Census Handbook-Rayagada 2011", Directorate of Census Operation, Odisha https://censusindia.gov.in/2011censusdchb/2127_PART_B_DCHB_RAYAGADA.pdf, accessed August 11, 2020
13. "About Malkangiri", Govt. of Odisha, https://malkangiri.nic.in/about-district/

    "Administrative Setup", last modified Sep 07, 2020, https://malkangiri.nic.in/administrative-setup/
14. Nabarangpur, "About District", Govt. of Odisha, last modified Sep 09, 2020, https://nabarangpur.nic.in/about-district/

15. "About District", Govt. of Odisha, last modified Sep 14, 2020, https://balangir.nic.in
16. Subarnapur, "About District", Govt. of Odisha, last modified Jul 22, 2020, https://subarnapur.nic.in/about-district
17. Kalahandi, "About District", last modified Sep 09, 2020, https://kalahandi.nic.in/about-district
18. The Niyamgiri hills are lush green ranges situated in the districts of Kalahandi and Rayagada. They are home to the tribe of Dongria Kondh, who find their sustenance entirely on the hills and worship their mountain god 'Niyam Raja' who is integral to every part of their lives. For over a decade, the Dongria Kondhs had to fight off interference by Vedanta Resources, a mining company, on their lands. The company wanted to make an open-cast mine that would have polluted their rivers and forests, and destroyed their relationship with Niyam Raja. The dispute over these issues reached up to the Supreme Court of India. In the year 2013, the Supreme Court decided that the forest rights vests in the tribals and the determination of customary, social, religious, traditional rights has to be made by the gram sabhas. [Orissa Mining Corporation Ltd. V. Ministry of Environment & Forest, (2013) 6 SCC 476].
19. Nuapada, "About District", last modified Sep 07, 2020, https://nuapada.nic.in/about-district

Poverty and Famine in Odisha

> Famine is India's specialty. Elsewhere famines are inconsequential incidents—in India they are devastating cataclysms; in one case they annihilate hundreds; in the other, millions.
>
> **– Mark Twain[1]**

During the pre-British period, most of the tribal areas of Odisha were autonomous. The British, on takeover, started to bring the tribal areas under the state's administrative control. This was immediately resisted by the tribals and very often, the resistance was violent, which, in turn, led to forced displacement and migration of the tribals.[2] In fact, the princely states as well as the Britishers attempted to impose administrative control over the tribal areas and to settle lands in favour of non-tribals. The 1882 Kondh rebellion was caused by the discontentment of the Kondhs of Kalahandi, over the king's decision to settle Kultas, a non-tribal agricultural community, in the region. The rebellion was brutally suppressed by the king with the support of the British. Thus, the sufferings of the tribals began when the local rulers (i.e., rajas) supported British colonial interests and denied the forest-dwelling tribes their rights to their lands and resources. In 1922-23, restrictions were imposed on the *zamindari* system. Forest laws (relating to protection of the forests) were introduced in the region, prohibiting the tribals from collecting wood and other forest produce. Communities who were mostly dependent on land and forest resources for their sustenance suffered a great deal due to the forced transfer and occupation of their lands.[3] This deprivation has to be seen in the light of the poverty, famine and drought which this region has faced for centuries.

The Great Orissa Famine of 1866 (known as *Na Anka*) was preceded by the drought of 1865. The failure of crops coupled with inefficiency and lack of foresight of the administration gave rise to a famine so severe that one among every three people died in the region. The administration, for its part, continued to believe in the Malthusian theory that the hunger-related deaths were caused by overpopulation![4] By the time the gravity of the situation was realized, and it was understood that import of rice was necessary for relief, the monsoon struck, rendering the affected area completely inaccessible. In a bitter irony, the drought and famine were followed by floods. Foodgrains brought in for relief lay mostly unused and were soon rotten. This exposed the brazen inefficiency of the administration in tackling such emergencies. Moreover, when people of the region were being starved and left to die, over 200 million pounds of rice were being exported to Great Britain. Many people died from cholera before the monsoons, and malaria afterwards. Across Odisha, millions of people died: about one-third of its population was razed. This great tragedy resulted in the formation of the Campbell Famine Commission (1866) and its realization that the development of roads, railways, navigable waterways and communication was an utmost necessity.[5]

Another factor responsible for this situation was the hoarding of foodgrains by unscrupulous traders. This increased the prices in the market,[6] which many could not afford. They went hungry. However, many of these deaths could have been averted if the transport of relief food was efficient. A lack of irrigation canals worsened the situation.[7]

Prof. Amartya Sen has rightly said that famines during the British Raj were not caused by the unavailability of food, but were the result of its unequal distribution. An imperialistic attitude of the colonial rulers pushed a large section of the Indian population to the edge of starvation.[8] In this regard, reference has been made to Chittaprosad Bhattacharya, an artist known for his sketches in pen and ink depicting the misery of the Bengal famine (1943). These sketches were published under the title *Hungry Bengal*.[9] The British government seized and destroyed thousands of copies of the book because it exposed the incompetence and apathy of the administration.

The impact of the famine was felt in the political, economic as well as the social spheres of that time. People who availed of food facilities in the relief centres during the famine were considered to be a new caste altogether, known as *chhatra-kia*. The 1866 Orissa famine was so severe that it introduced some new words into the Oriya language, as well as some new practices in day-to-day life in the region. For example, the inclusion of wild leafy vegetables of inferior quality in the diet.[10]

The vicious cycle of drought, famines, scarce resources and population displacement became salient features of the region. When a season of drought would hit and crops were expected to fail, farmers and their families would migrate to urban areas in search of employment. When this did not work, they would return to their villages, only to find that the prime time for sowing seeds had passed, culminating in no harvest for another cycle. Lands left uncultivated for long periods also became less fertile and this also affected the harvests.

In the Great Famine of 1897, the death rate was 81 per mile.[11] This was followed by the 1899 famine which was said to be of even greater magnitude. In the famine of 1919-20, the death toll was 80 per mile, mainly due to food scarcity. The famine and food scarcity in the region was repeated in the years 1954-55, 1965-66, 1974, 1979-80, and 1982-83, 1987-89, 1996, 2005 and thereafter in 2010 and 2011. The people of Odisha were thus perpetually in deplorable conditions owing to price rise, food shortages and the non-availability of alternative employment other than agriculture.

According to 'Open Letters' written to Lord Curzon, twenty-two famines were recorded in India till 1900 (within the 130 period of British Rule till then).[12] Incidentally, the first and the last major famines in British India occurred in Bengal, with the first occurring in 1770 and the last in 1943. The Bengal Famine of 1770 was a catastrophic one, with nearly one-third of the population estimated to be dead within nine months.[13]

The Report of the Indian Famine Commission (1878) tabulated the famines that took place in India between 1769 and 1878[14] :

Year	Area of Drought	Area of Famine or Scarcity
1769	Drought in Bengal	
1770		Famine in Bengal
1782	Drought in Bombay and Madras	
1783	Drought in Upper India	Famine in Madras and scarcity in Bombay
1784		Famine in Upper India from the Karamnasa to the Satlej
1791	Drought in Bombay, Hyderabad and Madras	
1792		Scarcity in north part of Madras, intense famine in Hyderabad and Southern Mahratta country. Severe famines in Deccan, Guzerat and Marwar
1802	Drought in South Hyderabad, and in the Deccan	
1803	Drought in the Ceded Province of North-Western Provinces and in Central India	Famine in Deccan and Hyderabad
1804		Famine in North-Western Provinces, and scarcity in Central India and Rajputana
1806	Drought in Central districts of Madras, from Trichinopoly to Nellore	
1807		Famine in Central districts of Madras
1812	Drought in Guzerat, Kutch and Kathiawar, and to some extent in Madras; also in Rajputana and Central India	
1813		Famine in Kutch and Kathiawar; intense in parts of Rajputana. Scarcity in parts of North-Western Provinces and of Madras
1823	Drought in Madras	

1824	Drought in Bombay	Famine in Madras, chiefly in the north
1825		Scarcity in Bombay, chiefly in Guzerat and the Northern Deccan
1832	Drought in Northern districts of Madras, except Ganjam, in the south of Hyderabad and the Southern Mahratta districts of Bombay	
1833	Drought in north part of Bombay, in Rajputana and parts of Punjab and North-Western Provinces	Famine in Northern districts of Madras intense in Gantur. Scarcity in Hyderabad and Southern Mahratta districts
1834		Scarcity in North Deccan and Guzerat, in Rajputana, the Hissar division of Punjab and the trans-Jumna districts of North-Western Provinces
1837	Drought in North-Western Provinces, Eastern states of Rajputana, and south-east part of Punjab	
1838	Drought in Guzerat, Kutch, and Kathiawar	Intense famine in Central Doab and trans-Jumna districts of North-Western Provinces, and in Delhi and Hissar divisions of Punjab
1839		Scarcity in Guzerat, Kutch, and Kathiawar
1844	Scanty rainfall in Deccan	
1845		Scarcity in Deccan
1853	Drought in Ceded districts of Madras, in South Hyderabad, and Sholapur and Kaladgi districts of Bombay	
1854		Famine in Bellary. Scarcity in adjoining parts of Madras, Hyderabad, and Bombay

1860	Drought in part of North-Western Provinces and Punjab and neighbouring States of Rajputana	
1861		Famine in Upper Doab of North-Western Provinces in Delhi and Hissar divisions of Punjab, and in adjoining parts of Rajputana. Scarcity in Kutch
1865	Drought in northern part of Madras, in South Hyderabad and north part of Mysore; in South Mahratta districts of Bombay, in Orissa and Behar, and all Western Bengal	
1866		Famine in Ganjam and Bellary districts of Madras, in Orissa (intense), and in Behar. Scarcity in all adjacent parts of Madras, Mysore, Hyderabad, and Bombay, and in Central and Western Bengal
1868	Drought in Rajputana, trans-Jumna districts of North-Western Provinces, north and south-east districts of Central Provinces, and in Punjab from Jumna to Indus	
1869		Famine in Western Rajputana (intense), in trans-Jumna districts of Allahabad and Delhi, and Hissar divisions of Punjab. Scarcity in adjacent parts of North-Western Provinces and Punjab, in Guzerat, Kutch and North Deccan, and in the north and south-east districts of Central Provinces
1873	Drought in North Behar and a part of North-Western Provinces and Oudh	
1874		Famine in Behar and scarcity in the strip of North-Western Provinces and Oudh adjacent

1876	Drought in all Madras and Deccan, Mysore and south part of Hyderabad	
1877	Drought in Central Provinces, North-Western Provinces, and Punjab	Famine in Madras, Mysore, Bombay, and Hyderabad
1878		Famine in North-Western Provinces and Cashmere. Scarcity in Punjab

The Report of the Indian Famine Commission (1878-80) was the first comprehensive exercise by the British government in India to understand the causes of famine as well as the ways in which they could be successfully dealt with. The report acknowledged that until 1878, the response from the administration had been far from adequate, which resulted in higher mortality during the events.[15] The report also concluded that these famines were not merely results of failure of rainfall or rise in prices, but the causes were deeper—enmeshed in systemic and structural problems.

The report was crucial because it was for the first time that the expected response and obligation of the government in the face of scarcity and deprivation was discussed. The report concluded that the steps taken till then to tackle famines were simply not enough and that the government should spend more, to address the problem effectively. The report also notably concluded that any expenditures on famines must not be viewed as a 'financial embarrassment.' It was recommended that Famine Codes should be drawn up for each province, and that the role of the government should not only be limited to providing public employment, rather, should be extended to 'gratuitous relief'! The report also suggested that the railway system in the country should be improved to ensure the distribution of food grains.[16]

These invaluable suggestions of the Commission, however, were not implemented and famines continued to occur. As a result, on 23 December, 1897, a fresh commission was established by order. Its report was submitted in 1898. However, it is interesting to note the scope of this new inquiry:

> So, too, the experience of the past year has shown that the general lines of policy laid down in 1878 stand in no need of reconsideration. It is the

details of the scheme of relief that require to be revised. But in such a matter details are hardly less important than principles.[17]

It was surprisingly observed that the overall power of the people to resist famine had increased![18] It was suggested that 'gratuitous relief' must be granted even during periods of rain. The report went on to conclude that it is not certain that the mortality which occurred during the intervening period between the two reports could be attributed directly to famines.[19]

Immediately following this report, and before the suggestions could be incorporated into the famine codes—another famine occurred in 1899. The report of 1901 laid down better warning signals, to watch out for impending famines. These were:

(1) contraction of private charity, indicated by the wandering of paupers;
(2) the contraction of credit;
(3) feverish trading in the grain market;
(4) restlessness, showing in an increase of crime;
(5) unusual movements of flocks and herds in search of pasturage; and
(6) unusual wandering of people.[20]

The report recommended that, while these may not be absolute signs of famine, their presence be noted and forecasts of famines be made.

However, none of this was enough, and Bengal saw one of its worst famines in 1943. This time's Inquiry Commission, which submitted its report in 1945, estimated that the death of about 1.5 million people was attributable to the famine. It was further confirmed that while initially it was thought that the cause of the famine was food shortages in 1943, the real cause of the famine actually was non-importation of food from neighbouring states as well as failure to avoid hoarding.[21] Historians, however, estimate that upto 3 million people died in Bengal alone out of a population of 60.3 million, due to famine-induced starvation, malaria and other diseases worsened by population displacement, lack of proper hygiene and healthcare. Historians and academicians consider the causes of famine as manmade—sourced to colonial policies, rather than natural causes.[22]

The problem in the KBK districts was summed up in the 106th Report of the Rajya Sabha Committee on Petitions (31 March, 1998) as follows:

The phenomenon of starvation deaths in the KBK region has been taken note of by various Committees from time to time and various reports have been presented at various levels in this regard. But the situation still persists in KBK areas. The area has been visited by many Prime Ministers of the country and they have announced many packages for the KBK region but backwardness still haunts the region. The undivided KBK region has been endowed with many natural gifts in abundance. The area has many rivers to get plenty of water. The ground water level is also satisfactory. The land is fertile and many areas are surplus in food production. But the area is suffering due to human failure. There is rampant corruption and human greed has resulted in mass destruction of forests resulting in soil erosion. The Central and State governments are implementing various schemes in the areas but implementation is in bureaucratic hands which have developed vested interests therein.

References

1. Mark Twain, *Following the Equator* (Hartford: American Publishing Company, 1897), chap. XLIII
2. See generally Shalini Padhi, Nilakantha Panigrahi, "Tribal Movements and Livelihoods: Recent Developments in Orissa: CRPC-IIPA Working Paper No. 51", *Semantic Scholar* (2011), https://api.semanticscholar.org/CorpusID:54693467
3. Rajya Sabha Hundred and Sixth Report of the Committee on Petitions on the petition signed by Shri Chittaranjan Mandal of Orissa pertaining to improper use of funds meant for poverty alleviation programmes leading to starvation death, in undivided districts of Kalahandi, Balangir and Koraput in Orissa. (March 31, 1998).
4. See generally Mark Duffield and Vernon Hewitt (ed.), *Empire, Development & Colonialism: the Past in the Present* (Woodbridge: Boydell & Brewer, 2013), B. R. Tomlinson, *The Economy of Modern India*, 1860-1970 (Cambridge: Cambridge University Press, 1993)
5. H.K. Mishra, *Famines and Poverty in India* (New Delhi: Ashish Publishing House, 1991), 136.
6. Amartya Sen, P*overty and Famines: An Essay on Entitlement and Deprivation* (New Delhi: Oxford University Press, 1982); Tirthankar Roy, *Were Indian Famines 'Natural' Or 'Manmade'?* (New Delhi: Oxford University Press, 2012)
7. Ganeswar Nayak, "The Orissa Famine of 1866", *International Institute of Asian Studies Newsletter,* No. 52, 2009, 14.
8. Sen, Ibid., *Roy,* Ibid.
9. Sen, Ibid., 52-85; Janam *Mukherjee, Hungry Bengal: War, Famine, Riots, and the End of Empire 1939–1946* (PhD Diss., University of Michigan, 2011); Nikhil Sarkar, *A Matter of Conscience: Artists Bear Witness to the Great Bengal Famine of 1943* (Calcutta: Punascha, 1998).
10. Bidyut Mohanty, "Orissa Famine of 1866: Demographic and Economic Consequences", *Economic and Political Weekly*, Vol. 28, (January, 2-9, 1993): 55.

11. Suvendra Jenamani, *Poverty and Underdevelopment in Tribal Areas: A Geographical Analysis*, (Delhi: Concept Publishing Company, 2005), 54.
12. Romesh C Dutt, *Famines and Land Assessment in India*, (Delhi: B.R. Publishing Corporation, 1985), 1.
13. J. E. Scott, *In Famine Land: Observations and Experiences in India During the Great Drought of 1899–1900* (London: Harper & Brothers, 1904), 3.
14. Report of the Indian Famine Commission (1880), 21-22. The words used in the Report are used here without alteration. For instance, Guzerat refers approximately to present-day Gujarat.
15. Ibid., 27.
16. Ibid., p.27.
17. Report of the Indian Famine Commission (1898), 2.
18. Ibid., 360-361.
19. Ibid., 196, para 339.
20. Report of the Indian Famine Commission 1901, (Calcutta, Office of the Superintendent of Government Printing, India,. 1901) 14-15.
21. Ibid., 103-108; Tarakchandra Das, *Bengal Famine* (1943), (Calcutta: University of Calcutta, 1949), 96-97.
22. Sen, Ibid., 52-85.

History of Famine Codes

The Famine Commission Report of 1880, which was the first important study by the British government on famines in India, had examined the factors that led to famines in the 130 years of British rule in the country. As mentioned earlier, the report notably suggested the passing of specific codes for different provinces, to combat famines. It was suggested as under:

> The duties involved in relief measures are complicated and multifarious; their successful performance necessitates the utilisation of large stores of accumulated experience and a carefully considered and prepared plan; they cannot be safely left to individual energy and resource, or be dealt with on a system improvised only when the emergency has arisen. Prompt and decided action in carrying out these measures is of primary importance, and by considering well beforehand the principles that should guide them, much of that hesitation and uncertainty of purpose, which have been found to be so detrimental in the past, will be avoided in the future. We recommend, therefore, that the Government of India should, as soon as possible, issue a set of rules embodying the main principles that should govern the administration of famine relief, and that these rules should be authoritative in all parts of British India.[1]

The Famine Commission Report of 1901 made further recommendations, based on which the Famine Codes were framed in provinces which did not have them or were revised.

Based on the Recommendations of the Commission, the Bihar and Orissa Famine Code came into existence in 1913 (it was revised in 1930).[2] When Odisha became a separate province in 1936, the Famine Code of 1930 was still active. After Independence, with the focus shifting to social welfare and economic development, it was soon realized, the old code was not adequate. Due to a fundamental change in the concept of grant of relief, several documents were issued by the State of Odisha to supplement the existing famine code, which included (i) Circulars and instructions on Flood Relief Measures (1996); (ii) Handbook of important circulars on drought-relief measures (1966); (iii) A compilation of circulars and orders issued by the Revenue Department (1972).

The Government of India, in view of the change in perception on grant of relief, also changed the principle of relief assistance to the states. The Report of the Seventh Finance Commission was published in 1978, based on which the Government of India (Ministry of Finance) revised instructions for financing of relief expenditure vide letter dated 25 April, 1979. In continuation to these developments, the Revenue Department of the State of Odisha amended the Orissa Relief Code on 29 March, 1980, to ensure that:

> No one should die of starvation but also to prevent physical deterioration and destitution of the people and to enable them to resume their ordinary pursuits of life on the return of better times and simultaneously to encourage the village community in making concerted and continuous efforts to fight a common misfortune.[3]

However, in the 1980 Code, the definition of famine was deleted by providing the following explanation:

> At one time 'Famine' was included as kind of Natural Calamity 'Famine' indicates a state of extreme paucity of food due to complete failure of crops consecutively for more than one year and acute form of human distress as well as acute distress to animals and birds on account thereof. With the development of quick transport and communication facilities and with improvements in the food production situation in the country, the conditions of famine could not be said to appear on any local failure of rains. Hence at present the question of declaration of any area as 'Famine Affected' does not arise.

The State found an easy way to escape its responsibility, to act urgently if an area was 'famine affected' by relying on the means of communication and food production. This *alibi* proved to be disastrous, resulting in denial of deaths occurring due to hunger, malnutrition and diseases caused on account of these factors. The reason why the Famine Code has not worked effectively to provide immediate relief to the people in distress is because of the bureaucratic hurdles involved in determining and declaring droughts. For example, Chapter III of the

Famine Code deals with drought. It is noted that the lack of rains in season and at proper times can have an adverse impact on agriculture activities and can hamper the growth of crops. The intensity of drought depends on the presence of the situation, that is, failure of rain, for many years at a stretch. However, as stated in the Code, a rain gauge station in every block should be checked by the Officer-in-charge of the Station. He would submit reports to the Collector and the Director of Agriculture & Food Production. The Collector then shall carry a review of the rainfall statistics and submit a report to the Board of Revenue by the 10th of July. Then, the Board of Revenue shall consider the report of the Collector. Next, the Board of Revenue/Special Relief Commissioner shall submit a consolidated report to the Government suggesting if any special measures are needed. Similar process was sanctioned regarding 'crop-loss assessment' which has to be done by Revenue Field Staff every year by 'eye-estimation' as per the resolution dated 3 September, 1977. After the lengthy process, declaration of drought is then done in respect of a particular area by the government, taking into consideration a crop assessment report submitted by the Collector and also the views of the Revenue Divisional Commissioner and the Board of Revenue.

It is only in exceptional situations that the government —without declaring a particular area 'drought-prone'—can pass on instructions to field officers to provide employment-oriented, labour-intensive works in selected distress areas. This highly technical and elongated method of a declaration of drought failed to bring any change in the KBK districts, and seemed to perpetuate starvation deaths and suffering of the people.

The Relief Code was updated in the year 1996,[4] and as it stands now, consists of 280 Sections and XVII chapters. The Code is now not just limited to droughts, but also covers other calamities which may cause a shortage of food including floods, cyclones, earthquakes, etc. Unfortunately, even in this Code, the method of assessment has remained the same. NHRC in its proceedings, as discussed in later chapters, has considered the limitations of the Relief Code to tackle the complicated problem of hunger and famine and also formulated principles and methodology based on constitutional rights. This has provided some relief for the people in KBK districts.

The Famine Codes have to be reformulated by the states, keeping in view Article 21 of the Constitution of India and the Directive Principles of State Policy, as well as the 'entitlement approach' which has been accepted as part of the 'right to food'.[5]

References

1. Report of the Indian Famine Commission (1880), 37.
2. Dan Banik, *Starvation and India's Democracy* (London: Routledge, 2007), 57.
3. Revenue & Disaster Management Department, Special Relief , *"Odisha Relief Code with Latest Amendments"*, https://srcodisha.nic.in/data/ORC-contents.pdf
4. Ibid.
5. PUCL vs. Union of India & Ors., (2013) 2 SCC 663. The entitlement approach was discussed by NHRC in its order dated 17.02.1998.

Hunger, Poverty and Famine : A Conceptual Framework

When hunger is persistent and chronic, it creates famine. Hunger is visible in many forms like malnutrition, chronic under-nutrition as well as lack of access to food. Famine is often connected with drought, floods and other adverse climatic conditions. These factors undoubtedly create distress in normal living conditions but they are not the only cause. As we have witnessed, "Famine has been produced throughout history not by nature but one set of humans withholding food from another in the face of local crop failure."[1] However, if a sound institutional mechanism exists, which ought to exist in a welfare state, disasters like famine cannot occur, though drought may. It is for this reason that in the present-day world, nobody talks about famine anymore, though it has not yet been obliterated. If a state accepts the existence of a famine, it will be considered without any further debate that the state has failed to carry out welfare measures. In the book, *Ending Hunger: An Idea Whose Time Has Come*,[2] significant data on the status of hunger that continues to exist throughout the world has been gathered. The facts are heart-wrenching.

- More than one billion people are chronically hungry.
- Every year 13 to 18 million people die as a result of hunger and starvation.
- Every 24 hours, 35,000 human beings die as a direct or indirect result of hunger and starvation, 24 every minute, 18 of whom are children under five years of age.
- No other disaster compares to the devastation of hunger.
- More people have died from hunger in the past two years than were killed in World War I and World War II combined.

- The number of people who die every two days of hunger and starvation is equivalent to the number who were killed instantly by the Hiroshima bomb.
- The worst earthquake in modern history—China in 1976—killed 242,000 people. Hunger kills that many people every seven days.

The book also maps out "the great hunger belt – starting from Southeast Asia running through the Indian subcontinent, the Middle East, throughout the continent of Africa and the equatorial region of Latin America". It acknowledges that 50% of the world's hungry people live in just five countries—India, Bangladesh, Nigeria, Pakistan and Indonesia." It recognizes that if hunger were wiped out from India alone, nearly one-third of the world's hunger would end. Though the above data is old, the situation has not changed much. India continues to perform poorly on world hunger indicators.[3]

The Food and Agriculture Organization of the United Nations (FAO) states that the world has not been generally progressing either towads ensuring access to safe, nutritious and sufficient food for all people all year around (SDG Target 2.1), or to eradicating all forms of malnutrition (SDG Target 2.2). From 2019 to 2020, the number of unnourished people grew by as many as 161 million, a crisis driven by conflict, climate change and the Covid-19 pandemic. As many as 811 million people still go hungry.[4] The report also affirms that "The world produces enough food for everyone." If the world produces enough food for 7.6 billion people, we cannot help wondering what creates hunger worldwide. The main causes of hunger have been identified as poverty, conflict, food and agricultural policies, as well as natural calamities related to climate change.[5]

The FAO recognizes three key factors that contribute to food security: physical availability of food, economic and physical access to food, food utilization and stability of these factors over time. In its latest report, *The State of Food Security and Nutrition in the World (2020)*, UNICEF reports that the world is not making adequate progress to achieve zero hunger by 2030. Moreover, the nutritional status of the most vulnerable population groups is expected to get worse due to the health and socio-economic impacts of the COVID-19 pandemic.[6]

But if poverty is the main cause of hunger, another question arises: Why are so many people poor? This complex question points towards a vicious cycle. At some stage, even hunger becomes a cause of poverty. Hunger affects the body and the mind, and it greatly affects the ability of a person to do any work for sustenance. Both poverty and hunger, thus, make one dependent on others/the state. Hunger and poverty are in one sense inseparable, though not equivalent. In some countries people are poor but not hungry. Poverty is more than hunger, for in some countries people are not only hungry but are also deprived of most human rights.[7] Hunger cannot be related only to the shortage of food or to the local crop failure. Hunger rises from absolute poverty where "its victims possess neither the resources to buy food nor control over the resources needed to produce it."[8]

In the context of KBK districts, it is both poverty and hunger. The problem can be presented thus: decades of poverty due to the lack of any dependable means of earning, landlessness or insufficient land for sustenance, forcible dispossession from the land and forest areas. These factors create chronic hunger, which results in starvation deaths, or compromises the immunity and the capability of the body so much that it cannot fight or protect itself from diseases like cholera, malaria, dysentery, etc. Before Independence, people in Odisha suffered due to drought or floods, aggravated by the culpable negligence of the British rulers. But shockingly, even after Independence—when the idea of a welfare state emerged which gave sanctity to human life under the Constitution—the state continued to blame droughts for the sufferings of people, including starvation deaths.

The judicial experiment in trying to understand the problem of starvation deaths clearly pointed to the apathy of the state machinery in providing relief to the vulnerable and poverty-ridden malnourished people, thus denying them access to food. The NHRC, in the initial phase of the proceedings before it (rightly) observed that it would not be realistic to attribute the human predicament of starvation deaths wholly to factors related to drought and scarcity. However, it went on to identify the key issue as being "lack of purchasing power of the affected population." Therefore, it saw the solution in introducing social security programmes which would increase the purchasing power of the affected people.[9]

However, a little later, in a further proceeding, after favourably quoting Prof. Amartya Sen, the NHRC was of the view that the shortage of income and purchasing power were not enough to explain starvation and that the focus should shift to an 'entitlement approach'.[10] The approach focuses on each person's entitlement to commodity bundles including food, and views starvation as a failure to be entitled to a bundle capable of meeting one's minimum food requirement. Prof. Amartya Sen summarized the entitlement approach as follows:[11]

> The entitlement approach to starvation and famines concentrates on the ability of people to command food through the legal means available in the society, including the use of production possibilities, trade opportunities, entitlements vis-à-vis the state, and other methods of acquiring food. A person starves either because he does not have the ability to command enough food, or because he does not use this ability to avoid starvation. The entitlement approach concentrates on the former, ignoring the latter possibility. Furthermore, it concentrates on those means of commanding food that are legitimized by the legal system in operation in that society. While it is an approach of some generality, it makes no attempt to include all possible influences that can in principle cause starvation, for example illegal transfers (e.g. looting), and choice failures (e.g. owing to inflexible food habits). Ownership of food is one of the most primitive property rights, and in each society there are rules governing this right. The entitlement approach concentrates on each person's entitlements to commodity bundles including food, and views starvation as resulting from a failure to be entitled to a bundle with enough food.

Prof. Sen concludes:[12]

> Finally, the focus on entitlement has the effect of emphasizing legal rights. Other relevant factors, for example market forces, can be seen as operating through a system of legal relations (ownership rights, contractual obligations, legal exchanges, etc.). The law stands between food availability and food entitlement. Starvation deaths can reflect legality with a vengeance.

Another interesting point which Professor Sen makes is that the Bengal famine of 1943 occurred "not only by the lack of democracy in colonial India but also by severe restrictions on reporting and criticism imposed on the Indian press, and the voluntary practice of silence on the famine that the British-owned media chose to follow."[13] He links famines to the lack of democracy thereby regarding democracy and freedom as being essential components of development. This argument, if applied in the case of KBK districts, it will come out that though democracy exists in the region, it does not function transparently. Democracy exists here without the ability to convey the correct facts and without allowing its actions to be criticized and challenged on the anvil of constitutional principles, especially those involving socio-economic rights of the poor and deprived. Recently, the need to have transparency and free flow of information has been affirmed by a nine-judge Bench of the Supreme Court by underlining the complementarity of civil, political and socio-economic rights.[14]

> Civil and political rights and socio-economic rights do not exist in a state of antagonism. The conditions necessary for realising or fulfilling socio-economic rights do not postulate the subversion of political freedom. The reason for this is simple. Socio-economic entitlements must yield true benefits to those for whom they are intended. This can be achieved by eliminating rent-seeking behaviour and by preventing the capture of social welfare benefits by persons who are not entitled to them. Capture of social welfare benefits can be obviated only when political systems are transparent and when there is a free flow of information. Opacity ensures benefit to those who monopolize scarce economic resources. On the other hand, conditions where civil and political freedoms flourish ensure that governmental policies are subject to critique and assessment. It is this scrutiny which sub-serves the purpose of ensuring that socio-economic benefits actually permeate to the underprivileged for whom they are meant. Conditions of freedom and a vibrant assertion of civil and political rights promote a constant review of the justness of socio-economic programmes and of their effectiveness in addressing deprivation and want. Scrutiny of public affairs is founded upon the existence of freedom. Hence civil and political rights and socio-economic rights are complementary and not mutually exclusive.

These observations correctly summarise that transperancy and free flow of information (without impending fear of criticism), are necessary to ensure individual's right to freedom of speech and expresion in a vibrant and healthy democracy; which in turn, paves way for realisation of social benifits and achievement of constitutinal aspiration of equality.

References

1. Asbjorn Eide, Wenche Barthe Eide, Susantha Goonatilake, Joan Gussow and Omawale (eds), *Food as a Human Right* (United Nations University Press, 1984)
2. Frederick A. Praeger, *Ending Hunger: An Idea Whose Time Has Come*, (New York: Praeger Publishers, 1985).
3. India ranked 94 out of 107 countries in "2020 Global Hunger Index by Severity", accessed on August 19, 2021. https://www.globalhungerindex.org/results/. India has a level of hunger that is serious.
4. The World is at a Critical Juncture, Food and Agriculture Organization of the United Nations (FAO), https://www.fao.org/state-of-food-security-nutrition, accessed on August 19, 2021. World hunger: Key facts and statistics, 2021 https://www.actionagainthunger.org accessed on August 19, 2021.
5. See also Frances Moore Lappe, Joseph Collins, Peter Rosset, with Luis Esparza, *World Hunger: Twelve Myths*, 2nd edition, (New York: Grove Press, 1998). The book debunks traditional notions of causes of hunger and establishes that land redistribution and other measures of equitable access have a stronger link with hunger than actual agricultural production. Therefore, hunger needs to be visualized beyond being an issue of insufficient food production.
6. *The State of Food Security and Nutrition in the World 2020*, UNICEF, https://www.unicef.org/reports/state-of-food-security-and-nutrition-2020
7. Urban Jonsson, "The Socio-Economic Causes of Hunger", in Eide & Others (eds), *Food as a Human Right.*
8. Ibid.
9. NHRC proceedings dated 17.09.1997 (Coram: Justice MN Venkatachaliah, Chairperson, Sh. Virendra Dayal, Member).
10. Proceedings dated 17.02.1998 (Coram: Justice MN Venkatachaliah, Chairperson, Sh. Virendra Dayal, Member, Justice VS Maliamath, Member).
11. Sen, *Poverty and Famines, 45.*
12. Ibid, 166.
13. Considered in Justice KS Puttaswamy v. Union of India, (2017) 10 SCC 1, para 269, (Chandrachud, J.).
14. Ibid., para 267.

International Law, Human Rights and The Right to Adequate Food

A brief introduction to the subject of starvation, poverty and hunger takes us to the efforts made internationally, in particular, human rights approaches to these problems. The UN Charter as well as the Universal Declaration of Human Rights (UDHR) emphasizes social progress, better standards of life and reaffirmation of faith in the dignity of human beings. Art 25(1) of the UDHR states, "Everyone has the right to a standard of living adequate for the health and well-being of himself and his family, including food...". It is worth noting that, in recognition of the Universal Declaration of Human Rights, a rights-based approach, which suggests that all human beings inherently have certain rights, has also been acknowledged by the International Covenant on Civil and Political Rights (ICCPR) as well as the International Covenant on Economic and Social Rights (ICESCR). Both Covenants were opened for signature in 1966 and were effective from 1976. ICCPR recognizes the right to life (Article 6), while the ICESCR covers socio-economic rights such as the right to work (Article 6), the right to social security (Article 9) and the right to an adequate standard of living, including adequate food, clothing and housing (Article 11). The ICESCR recognizes the Right to Food as follows:

Article 11

1. The States Parties to the present Covenant recognize the *right of everyone to* an adequate standard of living for himself and his family, including *adequate food*, clothing and housing, and to the continuous improvement of living conditions. The States Parties will take appropriate steps to ensure the realization of this right,

recognizing to this effect the essential importance of international cooperation based on free consent.

2. *The States Parties to the present Covenant, recognizing the fundamental right of everyone to be free from hunger*, shall take, individually and through international cooperation, the measures, including specific programmes, which are needed:
   (a) To improve methods of production, conservation and distribution of food by making full use of technical and scientificknowledge,bydisseminatingknowledgeoftheprinciplesof nutrition and by developing or reforming agrarian systems in such a way as to achieve the most efficient development and utilization of natural resources;
   (b) Taking into account the problems of both food-importing and food-exporting countries, to ensure an equitable distribution of world food supplies in relation to need.

Although the 'right of everyone to be free from hunger' has been recognized as 'fundamental,' its implementation has nevertheless been very poor not only in our country but in many parts the world. One reason is that civil and political rights have been given priority over social, cultural and economic rights. It is worth noting that the above-mentioned article has two basic approaches, the right to "adequate food" [Art. 11 (1)] and "the right of everyone to be free from hunger" [Art. 11 (2)]. Many scholars say that these two approaches are quite different, because the right to adequate food is broader and for practical implications, it should be taken as the primary norm.

> While it may be appropriate to focus on freedom from hunger as a means to mobilize public support and as a starting point for national and international efforts, such an approach should be seen only as the first step towards realization of the primary norm which is the right to adequate food.[1]

Art. 11(2) also indicates the steps which the state should take to achieve freedom from hunger:

(a) To improve methods of production, conservation and distribution of food by making full use of technical and scientific knowledge, by disseminating knowledge of the principles of nutrition and by developing or reforming agrarian systems in such a way as to achieve the most efficient development and utilization of natural resources;

(b) Taking into account the problems of both food-importing and food-exporting countries, to ensure an equitable distribution of world food supplies in relation to need.

The first major effort to give effect to Article 11 was the 1974 World Food Conference held by the United Nations where the 'Universal Declaration on the Eradication of Hunger and Malnutrition' was adopted. The causes of hunger were noted as follows:

> The situation of the peoples afflicted by hunger and malnutrition arises from their historical circumstances, especially social inequalities, including in many cases alien and colonial domination, foreign occupation, racial discrimination, apartheid and neo-colonialism in all its forms, which continue to be among the greatest obstacles to the full emancipation and progress of the developing countries and all the peoples involved. (UN World Food Conference, Rome, U.N. Doc. E/CONF. 65/20, at 1, 1974)

This was endorsed by the United Nations General Assembly in 1974. The above view was important in highlighting the socio-political context to the problem of hunger, compared to a technical stand alone assessment. This shift was also observed by the Food and Agriculture Organization of the United Nations (FAO).

> The causes of inadequate nutrition are many and closely interrelated, including ecological, sanitary and cultural constraints, but the principal cause is poverty. This, in turn, results from socio-economic development patterns which in most of the poorer countries have been characterized by a high degree of concentration of power, wealth and incomes in the hands of relatively small elites of national or foreign individuals or groups. (FAO, Annual Report, 1974)

In the United States, the Presidential Commission on World Hunger was established on September 5, 1978. The purpose of the commission was to investigate the problem of world hunger, by putting together factual data on the causes and extent of hunger and malnutrition in different parts of the world and making recommendations to help alleviate the problem. In the process, the commission reviewed the national and international existing programs, both private and public. The commission in its recommendations (1980) considered the 'right to food' to be the most fundamental of all human rights, without which the other rights have no value. The report noted:

> Whether one speaks of human rights or basic human needs, the right to food is the most basic of all. Unless that right is first fulfilled, the protection of other human rights becomes a mockery for those who must spend all their energy merely to maintain life itself... Unless all governments begin now to act upon their rhetorical commitments to ending hunger, the principle that human life is sacred, which forms the very underpinnings of human society, will gradually but relentlessly erode.

In this manner, the human rights approach to solve the problems of hunger and poverty dominated the international sphere.

Keeping up the said commitment, the UN established the Millennium Declaration and Millennium Development Goals (MDG) in the year 2000. These were a set of development goals that kept people at the centre. It was thought that in 15 years (by 2015) if the MDGs are properly put into action, poverty would end. At the end of the period, though it was found that the world had halved extreme poverty since 1990, and millions of deaths from malaria and tuberculosis had been averted, still there remained plenty of unfinished tasks. Keeping this in view, the "post-2015" Sustainable Development Agenda (SDG), a set of global goals was articulated in a UN report,[2] presented by the then Secretary General Kofi Annan.

The 17 SDGs mentioned in the report were adopted by all United Nations Member States in 2015. The first one among these aimed at eradicating global poverty while the second one was about ensuring food security and ending world hunger.[3] The report also pointed out six essential elements to bring these objectives into fruition.[4]

Under "Dignity: to end poverty and fight inequalities", it is noted in the report:

> Eradicating poverty by 2030 is the overarching objective of the sustainable development agenda. We live in a world of plenty, and at a moment of enormous scientific promise. And yet, for hundreds and hundreds of millions across the globe, this is also an age of gnawing deprivation. The defining challenge of our time is to close the gap between our determination to ensure a life of dignity for all, and the reality of persisting poverty and deepening inequality.

While addressing the Committee on World Food Security, on 12 October, 2015, at Rome, UN Secretary-General Ban Ki-moon stated,[5]

> Achieving Zero Hunger is our shared commitment. Now is the time to work as partners and build a truly global movement to ensure the Right for Food for all and to build sustainable agriculture and food systems.

The UN's 'Zero Hunger Challenge' has a mission to end malnutrition in all forms and to ensure access to enough food to everyone all year around. It recognizes that people have a right to adequate food and to be free from hunger. However, interconnected causes of hunger and malnutrition need to be addressed through an integrated approach of change to achieve a 'hunger-free world'.

The 2018 UN Report on SDGs[6] indicates, however, an increase in the level of hunger in the world from 2016, for the first time in nearly two decades; previously, the level of hunger was plunging since the year 2000. The 2021 UN Report on SDGs claims that worldwide, an additional 70-161 million people are likely to have experienced hunger as a result of the pandemic in 2020.

The right to food has been recognized as a basic human need and a human right in the UN Covenants. Besides, the duty of states to eradicate poverty has been enshrined in several other legal instruments. Most notably, the 'Beijing Declaration and Platform for Action' recognizes that poverty affects the majority of women and children in particular, and mandates that states must take steps to eradicate "structural causes of poverty".[7]

The American Convention of Human Rights, 1969, also called the Pact of San José, recognizes rights which are incidental to the right to food, such as the right to life,[8] dignity[9] and property.[10] The Additional Protocol to the said Convention, the "Protocol of San Salvador",[11] recognizes the Right to Food[12] and considers that the State Parties must improve methods to produce, supply and distribute food. Similar other human rights' instruments are also in agreement regarding the same issues. For instance, the African Charter on Human and Peoples' Rights and the European Convention on Human Rights (ECHR)[13] both recognize the right to life,[14] dignity[15] and property.[16] In fact, the African Charter also specifically recognizes the right to health.[17] Other instruments provide for this right in specific contexts. For example, the four Geneva Conventions of 1949 and their two Protocols of 1977, in the context of international humanitarian law, provide for the right to food of civilians and former combatants in time of war. Similar provisions for food and nutrition have been included for children,[18] women,[19] racial and ethnic minorities,[20] refugees[21] and prisoners.[22]

More recently, the UN's Food Assistance Convention, 2012[23] puts the onus on State Parties to provide food in cases of non-emergency as well as emergency. Further, the International Food Security Treaty Campaign (IFST)[24] recognizes that freedom from hunger is a fundamental human right and the state has the obligation to fulfil the right of access to food.

Internationally, different measures, conceptions and tools have been adopted in a shared dream to end world hunger, and to help people regardless of their caste and creed, gender, language, or geographical boundaries, to meet their nutritional needs.

Reference

1. Philip Alston, Barbara Harriss-White, Raymond Hoffenberg (eds.), "International Law and the Right to Food" in *Food: Multidisciplinary Perspectives* (Oxford: Blackwell, 1994), 205-216.
2. "The Road to Dignity by 2030: Ending Poverty, Transforming All Lives and Protecting the Planet", United Nations, (published December, 2014), accessed September 20, 2020, https://www.un.org/disabilities/documents/reports/SG_Synthesis_Report_Road_to_Dignity_by_ 2030.pdf
3. Goal 1. End poverty in all its forms everywhere.
   Goal 2. End hunger, achieve food security and improved nutrition and promote sustainable agriculture.
4. **Dignity:** to end poverty and fight inequalities
   People: to ensure healthy lives, knowledge, and the inclusion of women and children
   Prosperity: to grow a strong, inclusive, and transformative economy **Planet:** to protect our ecosystems for all societies and our children
   Justice: to promote safe and peaceful societies, and strong institutions **Partnership:** to catalyse global solidarity for sustainable development
   "The road to dignity by 2030: ending poverty, transforming all lives and protecting the planet" UN, A/69/700, accessed Aug 11, 2020
   https://www.un.org/en/development/desa/publications/files/2015/01/Synthesis ReportENG.pdf
5. Message of UN Secretary-General Ban Ki-moon. Committee on World Food Security, Rome, 12 October, 2015
6. *The Sustainable Development Goals Report 2018*, United Nations *https://unstats.un.org/sdgs/files/report/2018/TheSustainableDevelopmentGoalsReport2018-EN.pdf*

7. Article 26 of the Beijing Declaration and Platform for Action, UN, accessed August 11, 2020 http://www.un.org/womenwatch/daw/beijing/pdf/BDPfA%20E.pdf.
8. American Convention of Human Rights, 1969, Article 4
9. American Convention of Human Rights, 1969, Articles 6 & 11
10. American Convention of Human Rights, 1969, Article 21
11. The Additional Protocol to the American Convention on Human Rights in the area of Economic, Social, and Cultural Rights (more commonly known as the "Protocol of San Salvador") was adopted in 1988. available at http://www.oas.org/juridico/english/treaties/a-52.html.
12. Protocol of San Salvador, Article 12.
13. Convention for the Protection of Human Rights and Fundamental Freedoms, 1950.
14. African Charter for Human and Peoples Rights, Article 4; Convention for the Protection of Human Rights and Fundamental Freedoms, Article 2
15. African Charter for Human and Peoples' Rights, Article.5; Convention for the Protection of Human Rights and Fundamental Freedoms, Preamble.
16. African Charter for Human and Peoples Rights, Article 14; Protocol to the Convention for the Protection of Human Rights and Fundamental Freedoms, Article 1.
17. African Charter for Human and Peoples Rights, Article 16.
18. UN Convention on the Rights of the Child (UNCRC), Articles 24 and 27.
19. International Convention on the Elimination of All Forms of Discrimination Against Women, Article 12.
20. International Convention on the Elimination of All Forms of Racial Discrimination, Article 5.
21. Convention relating to the Status of Refugees, Chapter IV.
22. United Nations Standard Minimum Rules for the Treatment of Prisoners, 1955.
23. Food Assistance Convention (FAC), http://www.ifrc.org/docs/idrl/I1060EN.pdf.
24. Madeleine Schwartz, "Hunger Fighter", *Harvard Magazine*, Published June, 2011 https://harvardmagazine.com/2011/05/hunger-fighter

The Constitution of India and the Right to Food

Article 21 of the Constitution of India protects the right to life and livelihood. The meaning of 'life' has been broadly and liberally interpreted by the Supreme Court in several cases as including a meaningful existence, with dignity. The rights to shelter,[1] to a clean environment[2] and to potable drinking water[3] have been accepted as part of Article 21. In *Kapila Hingorani v. State of Bihar*,[4] hunger was considered as a violation of human rights. It is said that when there are resources available with the state, the right to provide food should be considered a duty of the state to ensure human dignity and self-reliance. The Supreme Court quoted the following from the *12 Misconceptions About the Right to Food (FIAN)* where it is *inter alia* stated:

> Is the Right to Food about good governance? Good governance is negotiable, Human Rights are not. The central concept for Human Rights is the concept of 'violation', referring to the suppression of vulnerable groups and individuals, whereas the concepts of good governance all too often deal with political theory and statistical indicators. If a country has the resources, but people get marginalized or continue in deprivation, this is not bad government, but oppression, intentional or not.
>
> Is the Right to Food realized if nobody is hungry anymore? Not necessarily. The Right to Food not only means that hunger and malnutrition are eradicated, but that future malnutrition can be eradicated by court action or other comparable mechanisms holding the state accountable on its obligations under the Right to Food.[5]

In the above context, the Court also referred to the judgment in *Kishen Pattanayak v. State of Orissa*,[6] dealing with the questions of hunger, poverty and starvation deaths. The Court also recalled the "Directive Principles of State Policy", (i.e., Arts. 39, 40, 41, 45, 47 and 48), which aim at empowering people to live and enjoy their Fundamental Rights including a life with dignity under Article 21 of the Constitution.

In *Shantistar Builders v. Narayan Khimalal Totame,* the Supreme Court considered the basic needs of a person as part of the right to life, and observed as follows:

> 9. Basic needs of man have traditionally been accepted to be three – food, clothing and shelter. The right to life is guaranteed in any civilized society. That would take within its sweep the right to food, the right to clothing, the right to a decent environment and a reasonable accommodation to live in.[7]

The Supreme Court has considered the provisions established in the UDHR, ICESCR and ECOSOC which can also be read into municipal law.[8] It also held that international covenants that represent the fundamental rights, can be read similarly under the Indian Constitution.[9] Even the Protection of Human Rights Act, 1993, acknowledges human rights as found embodied in the Constitution and International Covenants.[10]

It is, therefore, evident that the Right to Food is inherent to a life with dignity. It is necessary to read Article 21with Articles 39 (a) and 47 to understand the nature of the obligations of the state to effectively realize this right. Article 39(a)of the Constitution is fundamental in governance of the country. It requires the state to direct its policy towards ensuring that the citizens—all men and women–have adequate means of livelihood. Article 47 involves a primary duty of the state to raise the level of nutrition and standard of living of all citizens. Article 21 together with Articles 39(a) and 47–further emphasizes and confirms the importance of food security, thus making the Right to Food a guaranteed Fundamental Right, which, if infringed, is enforceable in the Supreme Court under Article 32 of the Constitution. Such a reading of the Constitution is clearly in tune with the obligations of the state as depicted in the ICESCR treaty adopted in 1966, to which India is a party.[11]

Going a step further, the NHRC acknowledged in these proceedings:

> The Right to Food implies the right to food at appropriate nutritional levels and the quantum of relief to those in distress must meet those levels in order to ensure that this right is actually secured and does not remain a theoretical concept.

Hence, food security must be ensured in terms of quantity, quality and availability.

Panchayats, as village-based self-governing bodies, can play an important role in alleviating hunger and poverty. In fact, Part IX to the Constitution titled "The Panchayats" and a new Eleventh Schedule have been introduced to help local gram panchayats improve the living standards of rural masses. It is a matter of serious concern that panchayats have not been sufficiently empowered to eradicate hunger and poverty, a dream which the Father of the Nation had cherished.[12]

In *PUCL v. Union of India & Ors.*,[13] the Supreme Court considered Article 21, which recognizes the right to live life with dignity and instructed that suitable schemes should be developed by the state for those living below the poverty line. In the said order, the Supreme Court has also spoken about the implementation of the Famine Code. However, this aspect needs a re-thinking because the Famine Codes in all the states were framed during the British colonial period, and have a very basic and rudimentary approach to assessing the impact of drought and other natural calamities on the people of the affected regions. There has been a fundamental shift from that approach, both internationally and nationally, and so today, the schemes have to be based on the 'entitlement approach', the only approach which is in line with the right to dignity guaranteed under Article 21 of the Constitution.

The above developments finally gained legislative recognition in the National Food Security Act, 2013.

> An act to provide for food and nutritional security in human life cycle approach, by ensuring access to adequate quantity of quality food at affordable prices to people to live a life with dignity and for matters connected therewith or incidental thereto.

Ensuring access to adequate quantity and quality of food should be based on the 'entitlement approach', which is non-negotiable. The implementation of the National Food Security Act, 2013 has been far from adequate. In fact, denial of food has found its way into statutory non-performance.[14]

Is it possible to bring in a change without disturbing the natural habitat, culture and tradition of the people living in these areas? Our Constitution promises fulfilment of basic needs—food, water, shelter and healthcare for every person irrespective of caste, creed, religion and sex. The poor and the deprived need a positive assurance from the government under welfare state principles and constitutional promises enshrined throughout our nation's fabric, particularly in the Fundamental Rights and Directive Principles. Policies to ameliorate sufferings of the people and their monitoring with transparency and accountability are the keys to real development. Starvation deaths, whenever they occur, are symptoms of the government failing in their human and constitutional duties. They, in fact, show, if not intentional, a culpable neglect of the right to food.

References

1. Shiv Sagar Tiwari v. Union of India & Ors., (1997) 1 SCC 444; Chameli Singh v. State of Uttar Pradesh, (1996) 2 SCC 549.
2. ND Jayal v. Union of India, (2004) 9 SCC 362.
3. AP Pollution Control Board II v. MV Nayudu & Ors., (2001) 2 SCC 62.
4. Kapila Hingorani v. State of Bihar, (2003) 6 SCC 1.
5. Ibid., para 50.
6. Kishen Pattanayak v. State of Orissa 1989 Supp (1) 258.
7. Shantistar Builders v. Narayan Khimalal Totame, (1990) 1 SCC 520, para 9.
8. Ibid, para 47, citing Chairman, Railway Board v. Chandrima Das, (2000) 2 SCC 465, para 24.
9. PUCL v. Union of India, (1997) 3 SCC 433.
10. "In terms of Section 2 of the Protection of Human Rights Act, 1993 (hereafter referred to as 'the Act'), "human rights" means the rights relating to life, liberty, equality and dignity of the individual guaranteed under the Constitution or embodied in the International Covenants and enforceable by courts in India. "International Covenants" means the International Covenant on Civil and Political Rights and the International Covenant on Economic, Social and Cultural Rights adopted by the General Assembly of the United Nations on the 16 December, 1966", NHRC, India, last modified Aug 8, 2018, https://nhrc.nic.in/faqs/how-are-human-rights-defined-protection-human-rights-act-1993-0
11. See NHRC proceedings dated 17.01.2003 (discussed below).
12. Under Article 243-G of the Constitution, the Legislature of the State by law can empower the Panchayats in preparation of plans for economic development and social justice and for implementation of schemes in relation to the matters listed in the Eleventh Schedule, which include agriculture, minor forest produce, rural housing and drinking water, poverty alleviation programmes, health and sanitation, welfare of weaker sections, in particular SC/ST, public distribution system etc. In fact, the Rajya Sabha Committee on Petitions in the 106th Report suggested that local self-government bodies be activated in KBK areas for implementing various schemes.
13. PUCL v. Union of India & Ors., (2013) 2 SCC 663.

14. For instance, making Aadhaar mandatory for getting ration has resulted in denial of food to millions, being also completely outside the scope of the Act. There has been a broader failure of States to comply with the provisions of the Act. See Swaraj Abhiyan v. Union of India, (2018) 12 SCC 170. The Delhi High Court in WP(C) 2161/2017, Delhi *Rozi-Roti Adhikar Abhiyan*, for instance, is considering the failure of the State to even notify the grievance redressal mechanism under the statute, after several years since the statute was enacted and despite repeated orders of the High Court.

Knocking at the Doors of the Supreme Court

After the integration of the princely states and the culmination of the colonial rule of the British, it was expected that the condition of the people in the KBK districts would improve. It was hoped that a welfare state now governed by the Constitution would take prompt action to relieve the pain and suffering of the people. Ensuring that people do not have to die of hunger should have been the primary duty of the Centre as well as the State of Odisha. They both have had mammoth machinery and infrastructure to execute the welfare schemes and also, sufficient money for the purpose. All that was required was a firm commitment and a strong will.

Unfortunately, these hopes were not fulfilled. Year after year, grim stories of drought and hunger in the KBK districts continued along with the news of people dying from starvation. The state, however, kept denying that the cause of the deaths was starvation. The Centre confined its responsibility to sending teams to study the drought situation and what—according to them—were the causes of the starvation deaths. The state formulated some schemes for the KBK districts but simply failed to apply them. When the executive failed to redress the situation in the KBK even after the making of the Constitution and decades of independence, what was left as the last resort was to approach the judiciary to bring some relief to the unfortunate people of the region.

In general, any intervention by the Court on such issues would be considered an example of judicial overreach. To look into the problem of starvation deaths obviously would mean delving into the nitty gritties of governmental functioning. However, the Supreme Court had already changed its approach towards the protection of human rights by entertaining not only cases of violations of civil rights and political freedoms, but also issues concerning socio-economic rights. This has been done by enlarging the canvas of Article 21 of the Constitution of India.[1]

I. Kishen Pattanayak makes the first attempt

In 1985, Kishen Pattanayak, a well-known thinker and social worker, along with Kapil Narayan Tiwari, another activist and social worker, addressed a letter to the then Chief Justice of India, pointing out the miserable conditions of the people of Kalahandi facing drought, extreme poverty and dying from chronic food shortage. The letter narrated how landlords exploited the poor tribals of Kalahandi and how 'chill penury' forced them to sell even their children. The letter was treated as a writ petition by the Supreme Court.

Another writ petition was filed by the Indian People's Front pointing out the pathetic condition of the people living in Koraput district. The petition alleged that people were dying of starvation due to the ineptitude and negligence of the Government of Odisha.

Kishen Pattanayak appeared in person and ably presented his case. The Supreme Court called for a report from the District Judge, Kalahandi. In a report consisting of 361 pages, the District Judge denied the allegations and indicated that there was hardly any case of starvation death in the region and that the government was running its social welfare schemes properly.

Both Pattanayak and Tiwari challenged the report of the District Judge by providing facts and figures that showed otherwise.

The State submitted that immediate actions were taken (in accordance with the Orissa Relief Code) as soon as the report of starvation deaths reached the Collector. The State also insisted that it had taken ample measures to improve the living conditions of the people in Kalahandi and Koraput. The following statistics related to welfare programmes carried out by the Government of Odisha were presented before the Supreme Court:

(i) Allocation of money for Kalahandi during the Sixth Plan—Rs. 8054 lakhs.

(ii) During the year 1984-85, in areas of acute distress, the state government undertook a free feeding programme extensively.

(iii) During 1987-88, the coverage under the Normal Feeding Programme was 2,12,800 persons. Besides 1,20,000 persons were also covered under the Emergency Drought Feeding Programme, where the crop damage was more than 50%.

(iv) During the *current year* (1988-89), the state government indicated the likelihood of crop damage in 74 Gram Panchayats and, therefore, covered 40,000 persons under the Emergency Feeding Programme and 2,12,800 persons under the Normal Feeding Programme. Under the Area Development Approach Programme for Total Backwardness Scheme covering certain blocks, about 20,000 persons were fed under the Feeding Programme. It was stated that in the year 1988, 2,72,00 persons were covered by the Feeding Programme in Kalahandi.

The Supreme Court, based on the above submissions of the state government, disposed of the writ petition. The Court in its judgment delivered on 9 January, 1989, noted that people of Kalahandi and Koraput are unquestionably very poor and are living below the poverty line:[2]

> We hope and trust that in view of the prompt action that has been taken by the government, soon the miseries of the people in these two districts will be over.

However, at the end, it made the following observation:

> "As prayed for by Shri Pattanayak, the petitioners are granted liberty to mention before this Hon'ble Court, if necessary."

The judgment of the Supreme Court did not indicate that the State of Odisha had a systematic approach in ending the suffering of the people on a short term and long-term basis. The relief programmes claimed to have been carried out by the state government were mostly ad-hoc in nature. There was nothing to show if the relief actually reached the affected people shown in the government's figures. The impact of the said judgment did not last long. The government failed to keep up its promises to the Apex Court and showed no zeal in solving this issue systematically and on a long-term basis. This led to another round of litigation.

II. Taking the issue forward: the second attempt

On 15 December, 1996, *India Today* published a shocking story titled "Endless Hunger", which focused on the scourge of poverty and starvation deaths in the KBK districts becoming a permanent phenomenon.[3] According to the article, Balgopal Mishra, an independent MLA from Balangir district claimed that a hundred people had died of starvation or related diseases in just two months. Chaturanan Mishra, Union Agriculture Minister, admitted that 180 starvation deaths had taken place in Kalahandi. The Collectors reported a 75% crop loss. It was deemed as the worst-ever drought to hit the area. The Centre declared the situation in the region a "national calamity". Kapil Narayan Tiwari—who petitioned the Supreme Court in 1989 regarding the ordeal in the KBK districts, made a grim remark again in 1996, that if the administration could not feed the people, it should at least "arrange a decent funeral for the dead." It was also revealed that successive governments, both at the state and Centre failed to deliver on their promises.

> But signs of famine can be seen throughout Balangir. In Talindar village, just 17 km from the district headquarters, Alekh Jhankar's family is still mourning his death. A daily-wage earner, Jhankar resorted to begging once famine struck. His four children would get a square meal occasionally, but Jhankar himself barely ate during his last few days, surviving on the thick muddy water from the village pond. One night he was gripped by a terrible pain in his stomach. He died soon after in the Balangir hospital last month. His children and wife subsist on the grain contributed by villagers for Jhankar's funeral. "After that finishes we will meet my father's fate," says 16-year-old Satya Narayan.[4]

In 1988, Rajiv Gandhi had launched the Area Development and Poverty Termination Programme. But this programme itself was discontinued after the V.P. Singh Government took over. In 1993, P.V. Narasimha Rao proposed a package of Rs.4,500 crore for the KBK project, which took yet another two years just to get formally launched. Shockingly, the Centre reneged on this commitment too. H.D. Deve Gowda was the prime minister during the period when the calamity struck the KBK region. The article recalls how he announced a grant of Rs. 50 crore after conducting an aerial survey of the drought-hit areas.

Although he had no time to land and witness the misery first-hand, ironically, he then flew off to Rome to address the World Food Summit, where he announced, "There will be no hunger on the face of this earth on the first day of 21st century... and in India I will lead the anti-hunger drive myself." The *India Today* article concluded that a prime minister, who claimed to be a 'humble farmer', should know that "promises do not fill empty stomachs".

It was certain that starvation deaths had taken place and continued to take place even after the judgment in Kishen Pattanayak (1989) along with the state's hollow promises and flagrant failure to use schemes and programmes which, if properly harnessed, would have long ended hunger and human despair in the area. Kishen Pattanayak had, by then, lost all hope of action from the government. Despite the Supreme Court order, he could feel that nothing had happened on the ground. It is at this juncture that four organizations—the Indian Council of Legal Aid and Advice, People's Union for Civil Liberties (PUCL), Research Foundation for Science Technology and Natural Resource Policy and the Centre for the Study of Administration of Relief (CSAR)—decided to file a writ petition in the Supreme Court, which came to be registered as W.P.(C) No.42 of 1997. It was filed based on the liberty granted in the *Kishen Pattanayak* judgment (*supra*) by the Supreme Court. In a letter Pattanayak said:

> Sale of children is a practice prevalent in these areas for a long time. Helpless parents sell their children in exchange for a sum with which they can buy a month's ration. They also hope that their child will become a tiny domestic servant in the owner's house. So they also feel obliged. Reports of sale of children in drought years must be looked upon as a by-product of scarcity conditions. In the present atmosphere of enthusiasm to stop child labour in the country the court must direct the Orissa government measures to stop new recruits of child labour in the drought affected areas. Not much can be expected by way of relief measures for the drought of 1996-97.[5]

The petition pointed out that the Bihar and Orissa Famine Code (1930) was revised and supplemented by the Orissa Relief Code (1980) wherein the definition of 'famine' was taken out and sub paragraph 3 of paragraph 2 was inserted.

The Orissa Relief Code (1980), surprisingly, denied the possibility of famines in the state, let alone giving guidelines for famine relief.[6] This was an important point. It was clear from the ground level situations in the KBK districts, that the people were constantly facing 'famine-like situations'—utter helplessness, loss of physical and vital strength due to chronic hunger, with nothing to hold on to. Hence, it was an extreme case of 'starvation' due to the apathy and the lackadaisical attitude of the government.

The petition pointed out that on one hand, the state government was refusing to face the reality that existed in the KBK districts while on the other, defending its actions on technical grounds. At the same time, even the Ministry of Agriculture, Union of India, which looks after relief administration, was only sending out teams to verify drought and famine conditions. The reports of these teams were never put in the public domain, and therefore, nobody knew about their contents. This is how the situation in the KBK districts has been repeatedly recognized and yet remained unmitigated for over a century.

The petition asserted that in a welfare state, it is the government's responsibility to act and provide complete protection to life as envisaged in Article 21 by following the Directive Principles laid down in the Constitution. It was emphasized that the Right to Food should be declared a Fundamental Right, to which every citizen of the country is entitled. The petition prayed for immediate action to relieve the suffering in Kalahandi, Koraput, Balangir and Nawapada and other deprived, famine-ridden districts of Odisha. It was also suggested in the petition that a report should be filed monthly before the Supreme Court to monitor the development progress in the affected districts of Odisha, and also if deaths occur due to starvation or famine-related causes, compensation should be paid to surviving family members or dependents.

The Supreme Court issued notice. The State of Odisha in its reply on 24 April, 1997, referred to the steps taken following the Supreme Court judgement in *Kishen Pattanayak* (supra). In para 14, the state government made a routine statement in order to explain the problems in KBK districts.

> In the State of Orissa, the districts of Kalahandi, Balangir and Koraput have often been in serious drought conditions mostly due to ecological imbalances and natural calamities.

After saying so, the state government also went on to explain how well it had responded "during such serious drought conditions and natural calamities." The state pointed out the Long Term Action Plan (LTAP) which was formulated to help people in distress. The government shrugged off large-scale migration woes by saying it was a "common phenomenon." The reply also contained data collected by the Special Relief Commissioner, Odisha, regarding deaths, which had reasons other than starvation. The logic behind this conclusion was quite disturbing.

i. In the case of the death of Danmudha Majhi, a 43 year-old resident of Nuapada, it was said that he had been suffering from TB. His wife and son were in healthy physical status and some utensils and rice were found on verification. This was the basis for assuming that it was not a case of starvation death.

ii. Dhaneswar Majhi (37 years-old) of Balangir, allegedly died 'due to high fever.' It was repeated that the physical health of the family members was good and that at the time of inquiry, some rice, mandiya, utensils, kerosene oil, two cots and cooked rice were found in the house.

iii. Similarly, Panu Naik, a 56 year-old man in Kalahandi district, was said to have died due to chronic rheumatic fever. He was survived by his wife, a ten-year-old daughter and an eight year-old son. A routine statement was made that the physical condition of the family members was good and that some utensils were found at the time of inquiry.

The reasons which were given by the Special Relief Commissioner to substantiate the claim that the deaths were not due to starvation, were neither germane to the causes of starvation nor comforting. This aspect was high lighted in the report of the NHRC team that visited these areas.

The Union of India (UOI) put its affidavit on record, stating that the state government is responsible for relief and rehabilitation measures in response to natural calamities, and that the Government of India only provides financial support to the state governments for rendering timely help to the affected people. However, the Union of India, instead of recognizing the famine-like situation, relied on 'eye estimation' of crop loss as a tool to assess famine.

> ...so far as the current drought situation in the state is concerned, according to the reports received from the Government of Odisha based on the eye estimation, 27,081 villages in 26 districts had sustained crop losses of 50% and above, and that after the crop cutting experiments have been completed, the total number of villages which have suffered crop losses of over 50% came down to 15,818.

The above responses of the state government and the central government laid bare their noncommittal and superficial stand in the matter of providing relief to the people of the KBK districts. The approach of using 'eye estimation' in the assessment of crop loss was derived from the days of the British Raj. This was highly impractical, unethical, and failed to address the root problem. The acute agony of the people was very much known to both the central and state governments. Relief could not be delayed or denied based on 'crop loss.' Blaming the environment and natural disasters was a brazen cover up for official inaction and administrative inefficiency.

III. NHRC Report of 11.02.1997[7]

Simultaneously, on the complaint of Chaturanan Mishra, Union Agriculture Minister, on 3 October, 1996, who also called attention to the starvation deaths taking place in Odisha, the NHRC was also conducting an enquiry. The official team sent by NHRC visited the districts of Nuapada, Kalahandi and Balangir from 11 to 17 December, 1996 and handed over its report to the NHRC on 4 February, 1997.

The Special Relief Commissioner had given a list of 50 deaths, which had taken place in Balangir, five deaths in Kalahandi, and three more, in Nuapada district. The NHRC team looked into three deaths in Nuapada, thirteen in Balangir and five in Kalahandi. For verifying the causes of death, the following method was adopted.

> (i) Visit the houses of the affected families and talk to the family members as well as neighbours and other village functionaries.

(ii) Ascertain:

(a) The extent of crop damage and availability of food-grains;

(b) Utilization of ration cards for drawal from the PDS;

(c) Level of wage employment in the family;

(d) Impact of relief measures such as Emergency Feeding Scheme, old/widow pensions; and,

(iii) Cross check the information on death with government records. In some cases, such cross-verification with government records was not possible as the health authorities did not have the record of all cases of death taking place in the village.

Based on these criteria, the NHRC team made the following observations:

> In the foregoing paragraphs, the Team has indicated its findings on the allegations of starvation deaths and also given an assessment of the efficacy of the current relief measures. It has also, on the basis of complaints received by it, highlighted some of the issues which need immediate and sustained attention. The team during its visit to affected areas witnessed *human suffering and destitution of an alarming magnitude.* It shares the *gloomy forebodings* of many that unless large-scale relief measures are expeditiously undertaken by the Administration, and vigorously implemented, the situation in the coming months is *going to further worsen* thereby causing very acute distress and suffering to the hapless people of the area. The Team earnestly hopes that such a situation will not come to pass.

Details given by the NHRC team regarding the starvation death cases were very shocking. Lives were lost due to hunger, not having any food for several days, acute under-nourishment, malnutrition and inability to battle diseases for the same reason. In sharp contrast to the previous claims by authorities that those were natural deaths, the NHRC team report revealed the real reasons.

i. Dhanbudha Majhi[8] of Nuapada was unable to find enough to eat as his son had migrated outside the village. He consequently died of starvation.

ii. Dhaneswar Majhi of Nuapada also died of starvation because the post mortem report indicated that there was nothing found in his stomach.

iii. Panu Naik of Kalahandi, who, according to district authorities, had died due to fever, was found to have had suffered from malnutrition, which ultimately caused his death.

The following were the details of the cases of starvation deaths in the KBK districts as reported by the NHRC:

S. No.	Name of deceased	Date of death	Village/ Block	Reported by	Observation
DISTRICT – NUAPADA					
1.	Dhaneswar Majhi (M) 37 years	11.10.96	Khamtorai, Khariar	State/ NP	The post-mortem report showed that he died due to some lung ailment, whereas other details in the post mortem report shown to the team indicate that nothing was found in his stomach.
2.	Rupobati Patel (F) 25 years	9.10.96	Gudbheli, Khariar	State	Govt. record indicates that death was due to some ailment, whereas villagers have asserted that she was without food for days together. Her father was without any job and unable to provide any food to her. Death seems to be due to prolonged malnourishment.
3.	Dhanbudha Majhi (M) 50 years	27.7.96	Mohulkot, Khariar	State	According to district authorities, he died due to natural causes but according to the villagers, he was unable to find enough to eat as his son had migrated outside and he consequently died of starvation. Version of the villagers appears true.
DISTRICT – KALAHANDI					
1.	Bucha Bhoi (M) 47 years	3.10.96	Jorabandh, Narla	NGO State	The deceased was reportedly undernourished and suffering from fever leading to death.
2.	Sahadev Suna (M) 63 years	18.10.96	Saplahara, Korlamunda	State	Family well-off, had productive cultivation and adequate food grains. Appears natural death due to illness.
3.	Surya Bhoi (F) 45 years	5.10.96	Talabhanra, Kesinga	State	Couple were beggars and had no issue. Deceased husband is blind. A villager claimed that he informed the BDO about the precarious condition of the deceased warranting immediate attention in Sept. No action taken. Death resulted due to prolonged malnourishment.

4.	Panu Naik (M) 50 years	8.11.96	Saurapadar, Kesinga	State/ NP	According to district authorities, death had taken place due to fever. Villagers who were present at the time of the Team's visit, however, asserted that the deceased (left behind wife and two children) had become very weak due to malnutrition, which ultimately caused his death.
5.	Khetra Mohan Joshi (M)	--	Tumura, Dharamgarh	State	Deceased was working in an aided school and had not received his payment of salary over a number of months. There was great economic distress in the family. Death was possibly due to acute undernourishment.
DISTRICT – BALANGIR					
1.	Nadhila Chhura (F) 60 years	6.11.96	Sindhekela, Bangomu-nda	MLA	Deceased, a widow, was staying alone and was in a state of destitution with hardly any shelter. Enquiries show that she died due to hunger and starvation as neighbours could not look after her in view of the prevailing drought situation.
2.	Balamati Naik (F) 45 years	6.9.96	Barlabahali, Bangomu-nda	MLA	Deceased, a widow, fell sick and could not earn her livelihood and died a slow death due to her hunger. Son (7 years) was evacuated to Mission Hospital in serious condition due to hunger. Team examined the child.
3.	Neta Naik (F) 60 years	6.11.96	Mahimunda, Puintola	MLA	Died due to T.B. It is learnt that some family members were also victims of TB. Deceased's nephew, Neelamani Seth (26 years) living, is also suffering from TB and is in bad shape. Death was due to ill health caused by undernourishment.
4.	Jaydev Bari (M) 75 years	25.10.96	Mahimunda, Balangir	MLA	Deceased, a widower, without any issue, appears to have died due to old age. Even his nephew is about 60 years old.
5.	Tulasi Biswal (F)	25.10.96	Randa, Puintala	MLA	Family extremely poor. Officials stated that she died due to illness. Her family members and villagers claimed that she died due to hunger. Clear inference could be drawn here.

6.	Betikhai Nag (F)	27.10.96	Randa, Puintala	MLA	Family in a state of extreme destitution with no earning member. From enquiries, death appears to be due to prolonged malnutrition.
7.	Sadhu Behera (M)	29.10.96	Randa, Puintala	MLA	Family in a state of destitution, totally undernourished, while officials stated that death was due to natural causes. Enquiries indicate that death was due to prolonged undernourishment.
8.	Sapura Bhoi (M) 35 years	9.10.96	Kutorla, Deogaon	NP	State authorities have shown death due to TB. Our enquiries indicate that the family is extremely poor and she being a widow was staying with her 60 year old mother. Death due to TB aggravated by undernourishment.
9.	Chera Naik (F) 60 years	30.10.96	Badhandh, Balangir	MLA	State authorities have shown her death due to illness, but villagers claimed that she died due to starvation. Enquiries indicate that death was probably due to prolonged undernourishment.
10.	Sukru Bhoi (M) 48 years	8.10.96	Chhotama-khan, Balangir	NP	He was a widower staying with his son (26 years), who is jobless. Family as such did not have any means of livelihood. Enquiries indicate that death could be probably due to prolonged hunger. Son is still without a job.
11.	Alekh Jhankar (M) 75 years	11.10.96	Taliudar, Loisingha	NP	Family claimed that he died due to starvation, but our enquiries indicate that death was probably due to old age.
12.	Bindira Motari (F) 50 years	28.10.96	Bhadra, Loisingha	NP	Deceased, a widow, was staying with her son who was unable to feed her because he himself was in a state of destitution. Enquiries indicate that death was due to prolonged undernourishment.
13.	Bironchi Khamari (M) 25 years	July, 96	Kandajuri, Loisingha	NP	Deceased, a labourer, was without any job and was unable to feed himself or his family members (wife and two small children). Enquiries indicate that death was due to TB and the ailment was aggravated by under-nourishment.

It is obvious from the details obtained that most of these deaths had taken place due to under-nourishment, prolonged malnutrition and hunger, except a few due to old age.

Hearings before the Supreme Court

When the petition came up before the Supreme Court for hearing on 28 April, 1997,[9] two different petitions filed by individuals on the same subject were being heard in the Odisha High Court. The Supreme Court, however, chose to continue the proceedings filed by the Indian Council of Legal Aid and Advice & Ors., as the main petition, by directing the withdrawal of the petitions pending before the Odisha High Court to the Supreme Court.

On the next date of hearing (21 July 1997), the Supreme Court took note of the matter which was pending before the NHRC initiated on the complaint of Chaturanan Mishra and said that further action can be taken after receiving the report of the NHRC.[10] It was also recorded that the state government shall carry through the directions of the NHRC, even of an interim nature. When the petitioner—the Indian Council of Legal Aid and Advice—suggested that certain interim directions are urgently needed to avert further deaths, the Court allowed the petitioners to approach the NHRC even for any urgent interim direction and also to give suggestions. It was thus made clear that the Supreme Court would consider the matter only after receiving the report of the NHRC. The Union of India was directed by the Court to appear and assist the NHRC in such a manner that the Commission would be able to fulfil its task. After this order, the writ petition before the Supreme Court was listed particularly for accepting the interim reports of the NHRC.

From 1997 to 2006, the proceedings continued before the NHRC.

After receiving the final report of the NHRC on 30 August 2006,[11] the Supreme Court took up the writ petition for hearing. In its order on 22 January, 2008, the Supreme Court accepted the NHRC Report in toto besides recording the statement of the state government that the suggestions of the NHRC would be implemented. It disposed of the writ petition by giving petitioners liberty to approach the court, if required.[12]

What is important in the story is the method and manner in which the proceedings began, and then continued before the NHRC, uncovering the causes of the pervasive suffering of the people of KBK districts, and creating an effective mechanism to bring about a change.

References

1. In this vein, it is interesting to note how this case led to the acceptance of the entitlement approach by acknowledging poverty and hunger as an issue of denial of human rights, rather than simply a policy failure.
2. Kishen Pattanayak v. State of Orissa, 1989 Supp (1) SCC 258.
3. Farzand Ahmed, "Starvation deaths, mass migration begin as worst ever drought stalks large parts of Orissa", *India Today,* December, 15, 1996. https://www.indiatoday.in/magazine/states/story/19961215-starvation-deaths-mass-migration-begin-as-worst-ever-drought-stalks-large-parts-of-orissa-834195-1996-12-15
4. Ibid,.
5. Excerpt from the letter of Kishen Pattanayak to the Author.
6. Para-2, sub-para 3 of the Orissa Relief Code (1980): At one time, famine was included as a kind of natural calamity. Famine indicates state of extreme paucity of food due to complete failure of crops consecutively for more than one year and acute distress to animals and birds on account thereof. With the development of quick transport and communication facilities and with improvements in the food production situation in the country, the conditions of famine could not be said to appear on any local failure of rains. *Hence at present the question of declaration of any area as 'Famine-affected' does not arise."* (emphasis added)
7. Report by Shankar Sen, Director-General and R.V. Pillai.
8. Though the spelling of name Dhanbudha Majhi on certain information may vary slightly in various reports, they refer to the same person.
9. Appendix A
10. Appendix B
11. Appendix F
12. Appendix G

Hearings before the National Human Rights Commission

The hearings at the NHRC commenced on 17 September 1997. They ended on 30 August 2006, after nearly nine years.

During this period, three successive Chairpersons dealt with the KBK issue. To begin with, Justice M. N. Venkatachaliah, followed by Justice J. S. Verma, and finally, Justice A. S. Anand—all retired Chief Justices of the Supreme Court.

The proceedings also saw participation from members of the Commission for different durations—namely, Virendra Dayal, Justice V. S. Malimath, Justice K. Ramaswamy and Sudarshan Agarwal. Among them, Virendra Dayal was the longest participating member—from 1997 to October, 2003. It bears repeating that the NHRC was already seized of a complaint filed by Chaturanan Mishra, former Union Minister for Agriculture, Government of India. In that regard, a team of NHRC officers had carried out a spot inspection of the scarcity-prone areas of KBK districts and had submitted a report to the NHRC, as mentioned earlier. The hearings held on 17 September 1997, 22 October, 1997 and 17 February 1998 dealt with the grant of interim reliefs to immediately address the grave situation in the KBK districts. They finally paved the way for long-term reliefs. So, they were considered at length. Subsequent proceedings covered the issues of hunger, poverty and access to basic means of livelihood, food, water, and health. They depict how each step was dovetailed for achieving a larger goal.

HEARINGS BY JUSTICE (RETD) M.N. VENKATACHALIAH (CHAIRPERSON)

Problem: Lack of purchasing power?

(Hearing held on 17.9.1997[1])

Following the Supreme Court's order of 21 July 1997, an application was moved on 1 September 1997 by the Indian Council for Legal Aid and others, before the NHRC. It relied upon the interim report of the NHRC dated 4 February 1997 and it sought several interim reliefs, including emergency feeding and medical care to vulnerable groups, provision of drinking water and provision of fodder to prevent distress sale of cattle etc.

In reply, the State of Odisha on 16 September 1997, *inter alia*, stated that 74,545 beneficiaries were covered under the Emergency Feeding Programme and received a daily ration of 200 gm of rice, 25 gm of moong dal, vegetables, salt and oil. The state asserted that enough food to last for 25 days a month was being stored at anganwadi centres.

It was not very clear in the reply if the beneficiaries were fed during the remaining 5 or 6 days. The figure of the beneficiaries, according to the state, in the year 1995-96 was 45,141 per day which increased in the year 1996-97 to 74,545 and the same was being continued.

This proceeding of the Commission was quite significant. The NHRC attributed the problem of starvation deaths to weak purchasing power:

> The problem of poverty and starvation has been a recurrent human problem in this area. Some of the earlier studies indicate that it is not necessarily one stemming from recurrent natural calamities; but the result of economic deprivation and lack of social opportunity. Indeed, some studies seek to point out that rainfall had, in fact, improved over the years in the area and so had food production. It is, therefore, not realistic to attribute the present human predicament wholly to factors related to drought and scarcity. *The key issue appears to be the lack of purchasing power of the affected population.*

The Commission urged the parties not to see these proceedings as 'adversarial' or 'contentious' and encouraged them to cooperate in developing a package of programmes—both short and long-term, which would actually help bring about a change. For the same purpose, the counsel for petitioners, with the assistance of the Government of Odisha, was requested to prepare a plan of action and submit it before the Commission on 25 September, 1997. As a result, a scheme for KBK was prepared. It included both long-term and short-term suggestions on various aspects—the Emergency Feeding Programme, food banks, drinking water, medical facilities, malnutrition, shelter, PDS, fodder for cattle, social security measures, etc. These suggestions from the counsel would form the basis for further directions by the NHRC. The beginning was very encouraging because the Commission not only recognized the problems of KBK districts as structural and systemic in nature, but also created an atmosphere conducive to identifying problems and finding solutions with mutual assistance.

Emergency feeding to continue

(Hearing held on 22.10.1997[2])

During this hearing, the Commission recognized the need for both short-term and long-term measures and also immediate need to grant interim reliefs. The Commission noted that till the end of September 1997, an emergency feeding programme was already in place providing food for 74,545 persons on a one-time-a-day basis for 25 days a month. This was done with the financial assistance of the Union of India. The Commission was of the view that the same should be continued "as it was before September 1997" until final recommendations were issued. The Commission believed that the feeding centres should secure rice at rates applicable to BPL families until further orders were issued. The Commission thus accepted the petitioners' prayer that no further deaths should take place owing to discontinuation of the Emergency Feeding Programme. This interim order prevented many deaths that could be caused by a lack of nutritional supplements. Meanwhile, counsel for the petitioners, as mentioned earlier, submitted a Plan of Action as desired by the NHRC.

Amartya Sen's 'Entitlement Approach' endorsed

(Hearing held on 17.02.1998[3])

The proceedings drawn up by the NHRC on this day were very significant and detailed. The hearing commenced with NHRC quoting Prof. Amartya Sen:

> Starvation is the characteristic of some people not having enough food to eat. It is not the characteristic of there being not enough food to eat.[4]

The NHRC took stock of the various programmes available such as the Emergency Feeding Programme, Old Age Pension, Disability Pension. Some other social security measures assessed were employment generation in the agriculture sector, economic security, social security, irrigation, drinking water, public health, land reforms, etc. Further, to understand the magnitude of the problems, the NHRC took note of Prof. Amartya Sen's 'entitlement approach' which focuses on:

> ...the ability of people to command food through the legal means available in the society, including the use of production possibilities, trade opportunities, entitlements *vis-à-vis* the State, and other methods of acquiring food.
>
> Sen further adds,
>
> ...Ownership of food is one of the most primitive property rights, and in each society there are rules governing this right. The entitlement approach concentrates on each person's entitlements to commodity bundles including food, and views starvation as resulting from a failure to be entitled to any bundle with enough food.[5]

The NHRC, in contrast to its previous proceedings on 17 September 1997, now endorsed the 'entitlement approach' which viewed food from a rights-based perspective, rather than a simple food availability decline (FAD), weak income or purchasing power. The NHRC referred in detail to the report of the Commission's team and to the comments made by the State of Odisha on the team's findings. It observed that the parties agreed to make "special efforts" to end the cycle of deprivation and malnutrition in the KBK districts. It stressed the need for a clear and transparent "practical programme of interim measures" which should be carried out with firm accountability and regular monitoring. The NHRC also doubted if the available schemes were really put into effect:

> It would also appear from the above that, despite all of the existing efforts and plans, it remained uncertain as to whether the "bundle of commodities", including food, which Professor Sen considered essential to ensuring that deaths did not occur as a result of starvation, was indeed available to all of the people of the 'KBK districts', especially the most vulnerable.[6]

The Commission, following the submissions of the petitioners, developed a practical programme for interim measures to which all parties agreed. The measures were to be applied for over a period of two years; periodic reviews could be held as needed. A glimpse of these programmes, and their data—will help us understand how, in the subsequent proceedings, the situation on the ground gradually began to improve. But before that, it is important to have a brief look at the monitoring mechanism developed by the Commission. The state government was expected to independently establish the details of a system of implementation and monitoring to curb the suffering in KBK, from the state level to the district level and below.

Mechanism suggested to make available the 'Bundle of Commodities':

- The state government would submit a specific set of comm itments—"district-wise and programme-wise"—on all eight districts of KBK. [The Commission noted that the state government had submitted the same for the period 1 December, 1997 to 31 April, 1998.]
- The state government would present before the Commission an appraisal about these programmes (time-specific) towards the end of March 1998.
- By 31 March 1998, the state government would also submit a "location-specific and time-bound plan" to the Commission for the months of May, June, and July of the same year.
- The procedure was to be repeated each following quarter which involved submitting to the Commission the appraisal of the previous quarter along with the plan for the next three months, a month before the latter began.
- The Commission would assess the progress achieved and give directions based on the advice of its Special Rapporteur, a notable person appointed by the Commission, while also maintaining the normal lines of command and control. The costs with respect to the Special Rapporteur would be borne by the Commission. The state government would cooperate with the Rapporteur and help him discharge his responsibilities.
- In these proceedings, the Commission also laid out the content of each programme and also the targets to be met. The specifics as pointed out were to be taken care of, as they would lead to successful implementation in the long run—both quantitatively and qualitatively.

i) Emergency Feeding Programme (EFP)

The Commission observed that 74,545 persons were being fed on a once-a-day basis for 25 days a month.

The Commission, after discussing with the petitioners and the state government, directed that this programme would continue; more eligible persons should be added; food offered should have proper calorific value, and expert nutritionists should be consulted for the same purpose.

ii) Old Age Pension, Disability Pension and Other Social Security Measures

The Commission clarified that all those who qualified for old age pensions, disability pensions and other social security measures under government-set criteria, would be included in the list of beneficiaries. The Commission referred to the state government's letter of 5 February 1998, which said that 47,959 more beneficiaries were added to the already covered list of 56,579 under the National Old Age Pension Scheme. Quick action by the central government was sought to fulfil the state government's proposal. Also, it was recommended that the process of distributing ID cards to beneficiaries should be expedited so that there is no delay in disbursement of pensions and other benefits.

iii) Employment Generation in Agriculture, Ecological Security, Soil Conservation and Other Schemes:

The Commission linked employment generation to several programmes set to be launched in the KBK districts. For instance, the Water Supply Scheme (which also involves the repair and maintenance of hand pumps), medicine supplies, soil conservation, irrigation works as well as afforestation works and water conservation, when implemented, would result in more locals being hired. However, the Commission also cautioned that those engaged in these employment generation programmes should be paid in a timely manner and delays of any kind should be dealt with by the state government's monitoring committee.

iv) Drinking Water:

The Commission referred to specific plans for 5 months, ending on 30 April, 1998 regarding drinking water supplied by the state government.

However, concerns were expressed on the conditions of tube wells and hand pumps which, the Commission thought, could be improved by training the local personnel and by improving logistics facilities.

v) Public Health:

The Commission noted that the state government's new regulations were in place to ensure posting of medical staff in rural areas. The Commission also recognized how miserably malnutrition affects young women and mothers, leading to an alarmingly low birthweight rate in newborns, which would cause the long-term loss of human potential. Iron, iodine and vitamin A supplements were recommended to be provided to young women in the KBK districts. The need for a health-cum-nutritional survey by an independent agency (for instance, the Nutrition Foundation of India) was also mentioned.

vi) Land Reforms:

The Commission recognized that land reform is a long-term measure but insisted that even at an interim stage, a committee should be formed to examine all aspects of land reforms in the KBK districts. This committee was required to give its report within a given time frame, and also to suggest how to deal with issues such as the lack of land reforms, the alienation of land, and migration.

The Commission clarified that the recommendations had been made following the orders of the Supreme Court of India and, so, the directions must be followed by the State of Odisha and the Union of India forthwith.

The above three hearings of the NHRC laid the foundation for improving the situation in the KBK districts and redressing the suffering of the people. Subsequent proceedings of the Commission, should be analyzed in light of these three hearings.

Performance Appraisal till 31.03.1998

(Hearing held on 27.4.1998[7])

The Commission considered the first performance appraisal for the quarter ending on 31 March, 1998 along with the state government's report dated 21 April, 1998. After going through the report, it was found that the targets had mostly been met. The gaps in the prescribed targets were added to the action plan for the months of May and June, 1998. The consolidated working plan upto June, 1998 was treated as the second quarter of 1998.

The petitioners insisted that there should be a time-frame for developing an appropriate land reforms programme and also that employment generation needed to be supplemented with a suitable afforestation plan. The State of Odisha agreed to present its existing plan of action on the afforestation programme in the KBK districts. The Commission added that an appropriate forest policy would help curb rural poverty. The Commission referred to the paper—*Forest Policy and Rural Poor in Orissa* by Dr. N.C Saxena, and acknowledged that non-timber forest produce provides monetary resources to forest-dwelling rural poor.[8]

The Commission directed that the report for the second quarter, ending on 30 June, 1998, shall be filed in the first week of July along with the action plan for the third quarter of the year. The Commission noted that the state government had already decided to involve the Nutrition Foundation of India (NFI) in conducting a survey in the KBK districts. Regarding old age pensions, adding to the directions issued in proceedings on 19 February 1998, the Commission now recommended old age pensions should have no numerical ceiling and everyone eligible should be added. The Commission also referred to the central government's concern over the funding of the Emergency Feeding Programme, but clarified that it is up to the central and state governments to sort out the arithmetic of the funding and that the programme should continue.

The Commission also expressed its desire to have the assistance of Dr. N.C. Saxena, Secretary at the Ministry of Rural Development, as *amicus curiae*. The Commission asked the petitioners' counsel as well as the state government, to submit within a week, the terms of reference, the checklist of items and the monitoring procedures to be followed by the Special Rapporteur.

Special Rapporteur to report on actual performance

(Hearing held on 13.7.1998[9])

This hearing mainly revolved around establishing the idea and role of the Special Rapporteur in relation to the action plan for the KBK and the corresponding performance appraisal report. The Commission assigned Chaman Lal, as its Special Rapporteur and requested him to proceed to the KBK districts to evaluate the execution of action plans till 31 March 1998 as well as for the months of April, May and June,. The state government was directed to render all necessary facilities to enable Chaman Lal to smoothly carry out the task.

The Commission also noted that the state government had failed to submit the performance appraisal report for April, May, June, 1998 which would now be filed by the state government in the first week of July together with the further action plan for the next quarter, (that is, July, August and September). The state was asked to submit this positively before the end of July.

Efforts to make the Performance Appraisal Reports meaningful

(Hearing held on 15.9.1998[10])

During this hearing, the Commission went through the performance appraisal of the action plan for the second quarter till June, and also looked into the action plan submitted by the State of Odisha for the next quarter (July-September, 1998).

The Commission considered petitioners' view that the action plans did not give a clear picture and also did not furnish particulars in a verifiable manner. Dr. Rangasamy—one of the petitioners—also argued that the purpose of performance appraisal would be defeated if both the action plan and performance review are not framed in a familiar and tested pro forma. The Commission was unsure if the targets in the action plans would be met within the expected time frame because there already was a heap of incomplete work across three action plans—for the periods December, 1997-April, 1998; May-June, 1998 and July-September 1998. The Commission expressed its hope that in the next action plan (October,-December, 1998) the backlog would be cleared. To make the whole exercise of performance appraisal reports and action plans meaningful, and to make sure that they did not remain only on paper but also could be translated into action at ground level, the following recommendations were made:

i) The Action Plan for the Quarter—October, November, December, 1998—should contain the backlog of various tasks accumulated in the previous plans along with fresh targets for the next term. It was also necessary to involve the heads of the district administration in preparing the action plans to strengthen their commitment to implementation.

ii) The Action Plan should also indicate the estimated financial outlays for each category of development works, and if necessary, would also point out what parts of them would be borne by the central government and the state government.

iii) The Performance Appraisal Reports should, besides other usual particulars, indicate the gaps in achievement in terms of money and as a percentage of the original estimate.

iv) Under employment generation, besides the achievement in terms of man-days generation, there should also be a record of numerical particulars of the number of families below the poverty line, who had employment-assurance.

v) The proceedings of the state-level committee overseeing the implementation, headed by the Chief Secretary, should be made a part of the Performance Appraisal Reports.

vi) The senior-level officers of the state should inspect from time to time the progress of works in different districts and blocks. The particulars of such visits must find a place in the Performance Appraisal Reports.

vii) The Action Plan for the months of October,-December, 1998 should be filed before the Commission by 10 October, 1998.

The state government agreed to submit information about afforestation, land reforms and a survey of nutritional status to the Commission on the next date. The Commission also directed the state government to make a particular location in KBK available to the Special Rapporteur Chaman Lal as it would help in evaluating the actual progress.

Focus on basic needs and essential services

(Hearing held on 3.11.1998[11])

During this hearing, the Commission went through the district-wise performance appraisal report submitted by the State of Odisha for the quarter July-September along with the action plan for the quarter October, December, 1998. The Special Rapporteur, who had visited four districts—Kalahandi, Nuapada, Sonepur and Balangir, also submitted his report. After seeing the reports and hearing the parties, the Commission felt that the relief programmes should have been faster and more extensive.

Among other suggestions, the Commission insisted that the action plans should be developed in consultation with respective district collectors and that the state-level monitoring committee, headed by the Chief Secretary, should meet more often and monitor the actual achievement of the targets as envisaged in the action plan. The Commission observed that the state should give attention to emergency feeding, public distribution system, drinking water, public health and pension schemes, and put forward the following recommendations :

- ❖ Emergency feeding and mid-day meal programmes should be strengthened. The daily programmes should be run uninterruptedly by ensuring adequate stock of food grains, etc., and requisite staff.
- ❖ Review the entitlements under the Public Distribution System (PDS) with a view to cover all persons who are recipients of Non-Commutable Allocated Pension (NCAP), State Old Age Pension (SOAP) and Odisha Disability Pension (ODP) to entitle them to draw rations at subsidized rates.
- ❖ Existing scale of one tube well for a population of 250 was to be reviewed along with relating it to population density, and as a result, providing a tube-well for 150 population in less populated areas. This was done to reduce the distance of reaching potable water from the existing one and a half kilometre to half kilometre. Importance was also placed on maintenance checks and repair of existing tubewells to keep them in good condition. Locals would be entrusted with minor repairs and upkeep and major repairs were to be carried out by the skilled cadre expeditiously within 24 hours of the reporting of the fault.
- ❖ Vacancies of doctors, paramedical and supporting staff in the hospitals and mobile health units should be filled up and the faulty equipment, vans etc., should be repaired and ready without any delays. Additional mobile healthcare units proposed for

various districts of the KBK region should soon be formed and made use of.

- Payment of pension under NCAP, SOAP, ODP should be done regularly every month and should be reflected on the identity cards issued to the pension holder. The Special Rapporteur came to know that, quite often, pension was not disbursed for months together. Similarly, employment generation under Jawahar Rozgar Yojna (JRY), Million Wells Scheme (MWS), Indira Awaas Yojana (IAY) should be made more systematic by identifying vulnerable families village-wise to give them their due share.
- The Commission asked the State of Odisha to speed up the programmes related to land reforms, afforestation projects, soil conservation projects and literacy. The Commission asked the Special Rapporteur to visit the remaining four KBK districts, i.e., Koraput, Malkangiri, Nabarangpur and Rayagada in the current month. The state government was also asked to submit a cumulative performance appraisal for the whole year starting from December, 1997 to December, 1998 regarding objectives achieved and targets unmet. The next action plan for the quarter January,-March 1999 was to be submitted before the Commission by 15 January, 1999.

Some hope, some disappointments

(Hearing held on 28.1.1999[12])

At this hearing, the Commission considered the following reports:

i) The district-wise Performance Appraisal Report for the quarter October, to December, 1998 and Action Plan for January, to March 1999, submitted by the state government;

ii) Consolidated Performance Appraisal Report for the period December, 1997 to December, 1998 in relation to Rural Development programmes, (JRY, EAS, IAY, MWS) RWS & Public Health Care; and,

iii) The Report of the Special Rapporteur, Chaman Lal, in relation to his visit to the remaining KBK districts (Koraput, Malkangiri, Sonepur, Rayagada) from 10 to 17 November, 1998.

The Special Rapporteur made a presentation of his observations about the extent, pace and quality of various relief and development activities in progress in the KBK districts. Through this presentation, the Commission noticed a definite improvement in the implementation of the RWS programme as well as pension programmes such as NCAP, SOAP and ODP. The Commission expressed its satisfaction at progress achieved. It was found that the pensioners had started availing PDS rice and the emergency feeding programme was improving, along with the Supplementary Nutrition Programme (SNP/CARE) and the Mid-Day Meal Scheme. The Commission emphasized that these programmes should be continued with the care of District Collectors to avert delays like the ones that took place in the past.

After considering the performance appraisal report related to afforestation activities, the Commission, while accepting the contention of the counsel for the petitioners, noted that the reports merely showed routine annual programmes of afforestation which had no relevance to the starvation deaths in the KBK districts with which the Commission was concerned. The state agreed to prepare and submit a fresh afforestation programme.

The Commission expressed its dissatisfaction over the failure of the state government in ensuring progress in soil conservation programmes. Referring to the report of the Special Rapporteur, it noted that the progress shown by the state from December, 1997 was only related to minor projects under EAS. No departmental works were taken up after December, 1997 under the National Watershed Development Programme for Rainfed Areas (NWDPRA), the Drought Prone Areas Programme (DPAP) and the Integrated Wastelands Development Programme (IWDP). The Commission gave some directions to successfully implement various schemes pertaining to drinking water, health, emergency feeding, PDS and pension, as follows:

i) Though the Rural Water Supply (RWS) programme targets were achieved, additional tube wells should be installed on 'actual need basis' in consultation with District Collectors, especially keeping in mind the needs of dalits and underprivileged persons living on the outskirts of the village. The Commission further noted that though maintenance of tube wells was reported to have improved, the state, as suggested by the Commission earlier, must ensure the involvement of local residents for the upkeep of the tube-wells.

ii) The Commission noted that though the state-sanctioned eight Public Health Centres six months ago in Koraput, Malkangiri, Kalahandi, Rayagada, they had not yet been operational due to a lack of posting of staff. Therefore, the state government was directed to immediately arrange staff through incentives and a tenure policy that rotated them to easier duty stations. Required facilities for these units, and suitable buildings for additional units also must be set up.

iii) The Commission directed the state to issue passbooks to the pensioners showing the pensioners' photograph and particulars of the pension disbursement in all the KBK districts.

iv) The Commission directed the state to upgrade the amount of items for the Emergency Feeding Programme (EFP), from 200 gm rice and 25 gm dal (lentil) to 250 gm rice and 40 gm dal (lentil) per head. The Commission urged the government to ensure that no area which needed emergency feeding should be left out as the said scheme was designed to battle starvation.

v) The Commission noted the existence of fake/ghost ration cards in certain areas and directed the state government to fix accountability on the persons/officials responsible for the issue of such cards.

vi) The Commission suggested that programmes—such as JRY and EAS—should be reported clearly, indicating the vulnerable families qualified to be benefitted under these schemes, and that the data should not be presented in terms of man-days only.

vii) The Commission noted the popularity and effectiveness of IAY and observed that this scheme should be applied by properly identifying the rural poor and granting benefits based on the recommendations of *palli sabha* at village level. In this case too, the Commission suggested that the state should issue passbooks to the beneficiaries clearly indicating date-wise details of disbursement of funds. About the RWS programme, it was added that the state should properly identify the beneficiaries and in case it was difficult to dig tube wells because of the nature of terrain in some places, the work should be done by the beneficiaries themselves. This would ensure that even the labour cost goes to the beneficiary.

The state agreed to draft and submit appropriate proposals/ programmes in respect of soil conservation, afforestation including minor forest produce, land reforms, health-cum-nutritional survey, and literacy.

Improvement in nutritional and health status

(Hearing held on 9.6.1999[13])

This hearing is important for several reasons. Besides reviewing the standard performance appraisal report and action plans, the Commission considered two other reports—a report dated 19 April, 1999 depicting the measures by the state government on the interim report of the Expert Committee on Land Reforms, and a report on the diet and nutritional situation in the KBK districts of Odisha produced by the National Institute of Nutrition, Hyderabad.

After hearing the Special Rapporteur—who had visited the concerned KBK districts—the Commission noted that, for the first time, mobile health units had started functioning, keeping one mobile health unit for each block (for 80 blocks of the KBK districts). The other important achievement recorded by the Commission was that the state government had decided to follow the advice of the National Institute of Nutrition and increase the quantity of dal from 25 gm to 40 gm in the EFPs and had also noted the proposal of the Secretary, Department of Women and Child Development, to substitute wheat with ragi. The Commission said that these decisions should be approved by the competent authority and implemented at the earliest. However, the Commission was skeptical about past claims of achievements in the health sector, considering the continuing prevalence of communicable diseases, and vacancies in posts for doctors, and recommended a systematic study of past efforts. It also recommended reports on irregularities in the application of social security schemes, on the health and nutritional status, on landholding patterns, and plans on afforestation and on literacy programmes.

The Commission hoped that the target of one tube well per 250 population would be achieved in all the districts within the year 1999-2000. The Commission also considered the interim report of the Expert Committee on Land Reforms and noted that a survey in Balangir district confirmed the widely held view that the distribution of surplus land, i.e., jagiri land, ceiling surplus land and government land had not done much to bring about the desired change in the pattern of land relationships in the rural areas. The interim report highlighted the need for vigorous action to deal with the problems of land alienation and rural indebtedness, which remained the patent causes of poverty and deprivation among SCs and STs. The Commission took note of the government's instructions to the District Collectors to check illegal land alienation and hoped that such a circular would yield concrete results including restoration of illegally alienated land to its rightful owners.

The Commission recommended that an increase in cultivable area, increase in yield, crop diversification and visible impact on material status of the beneficiaries should be taken as indicators while evaluating programmes. The Commission also recommended that the watershed treatment project undertaken at village Kendupati in Junagarh tehsil of Kalahandi district be treated as a model for other districts to follow.

KBK districts get drinking water, medical care and implementation of long-term land reform measures

(Hearing held on 22.3.2000[14])

The Commission considered the following reports in its hearing held on 22 March 2000:

i) The district-wise Performance Appraisal Report for the quarters April,-June, 1999 with Action Plan for July-September, 1999;

ii) The district-wise Performance Appraisal Report for the quarter July-September 1999 with Action Plan for October,-December, 1999;

iii) Report of Chaman Lal, Special Rapporteur, on his visit to KBK districts region from 26 December, 1999 to 6 January, 2000 and,

iv) The Compliance Report received from the government of Odisha on the issues raised by the Special Rapporteur in his report.

After going through the presentation made by the Special Rapporteur, and comments by the petitioners, the Commission praised the developments that had taken place under different heads. Regarding Rural Water Supply and Sanitation (RWSS), the Commission recorded that there was 100% achievement of the target of 'one tube well for 250 population' in the districts of Kalahandi, Balangir, Sonepur and Nuapada. It was hoped that the same target could be achieved in the remaining districts by 31 March, 2000, with an extension till 30 June, 2000 for difficult terrain, where sanitary wells were to be provided instead. The Commission also looked into the supply of piped water in six villages of Nuapada district and directed that the work be taken up on priority basis. In order to ensure that the tube wells installed were regularly maintained and repaired, the Commission emphasized that the scheme of 'self-employed mechanics' be implemented in a phased manner in all the KBK districts the way it has been done in the districts of Kalahandi and Balangir.

From the reports, it also emerged that medical and paramedical staff was now available in all the districts of KBK except Nuapada. The Commission was also concerned by the increasing incidents of deaths due to malaria in the KBK districts and sought an objective assessment of the existing anti malarial measures, and effective strategies to tackle the same.

The Commission noted that the involvement of Gram Panchayats brought improvement in the functioning of the PDS. To make the Emergency Feeding Programme effective in remotely located blocks such as Chandrapur, Ramaguda and Kashipur of Rayagada district, the Commission said that an alternative scheme should be examined involving the supply of dry ration to the affected persons who are unable to walk to the feeding centres for a daily meal. In addition, the Commission asked the state government to extend door-step delivery of food material in some places.

The subject of land reforms—which fell within the Long Term Action Plan—was considered following the expert committee's recommendations.

Tightening enforcement and improving the implementation of existing land reforms was required with some changes to make them more effective. On the question of alienation of land—an important measure to combat the existing situation in KBK— the Commission noted that the Prime Minister had written a letter to the Chief Minister of Odisha about the inadequacy of the existing revenue laws in the state to tackle the problem of large scale alienation of agricultural land from tribal to non-tribal communities. The state was also urged to consider legislative intervention to put an end to this chronic problem by examining the relevant provisions of revenue laws of Madhya Pradesh and Andhra Pradesh.

The Commission acknowledged the affidavit from the State of Odisha seeking to file a blueprint of its pro-poor policy regarding minor forest produce, and directed the state-level Committee to monitor the progress at various levels.

With the above observations and recommendations, the Commission directed the State of Odisha to submit a consolidated report on the achievements under various heads for the period January, 1998-March 2000. The Commission needed this because it wished to dovetail the short-term corrective measures into its long-term plans to find a permanent solution to the problems of the KBK districts.

These proceedings were the last one during the tenure of Justice Venkatachaliah who had laid the foundation of these proceedings and given it a meaningful direction.

HEARINGS BY JUSTICE (RETD) J.S. VERMA CHAIRPERSON

Taking stock of the situation; emphasis on monitoring and long-term measures

(Hearing held on 14.12.2000[15])

After Justice M.N. Venkatachaliah completed his tenure as the chairperson of the NHRC, Justice J.S. Verma took over and continued the proceedings with the same enthusiasm. He decided to take stock of the situation, to know the impact of the proceedings on the ground.

In this hearing, the Commission considered:

i) The district-wise Performance Appraisal Report for the quarter January,-March 2000 submitted by the state government;

ii) The district-wise consolidated report for the period January, 1998 to March 2000 submitted by the state government;
iii) The Report of the Special Rapporteur about his visit to KBK districts and Bhubaneshwar between 7-17 August 2000; and
iv) The Compliance Report dated 8 December, 2000 from the state government regarding the points raised by the Special Rapporteur in his report.

Upon hearing the parties, considering the suggestions of the counsel for the petitioners and appreciating the presentation made by the Special Rapporteur, the Commission made the following observations and issued appropriate directions:

i. Rural Water Supply and Sanitation

The Commission noted the achievement of the Government of Odisha in meeting the target of 'one tube well for 250 population' within the stipulated time frame, except in Koraput district. Considering the difficulty associated with the terrain in this district, the Commission granted time till 31 March 2001 for the state to achieve the target which had been set for the area.

The Commission recorded unsatisfactory repair and maintenance of water installations at Malkangiri, Balangir and Subarnapur as well as poor implementation of the Self-Employed Mechanics (SEM) scheme in many districts.

The Commission further took note of the delay in commissioning the piped water supply scheme in six villages of Karlakot Gram Panchayat in Nuapada district—as recorded in the proceedings held on 22 March 2000—and expected an assurance including a time frame from the state government in taking action and including it in the Action Taken Report.

The Commission directed the state to ensure that the District Magistrates review the existing arrangement after 'one tube well for 250 population' is implemented considering water source is available within 1.6 km in the plains and 100 meters elevation difference in the hills.

ii. Primary Health Care

The Commission took note of the opening of eight additional PHCs and 49 additional mobile health units in KBK districts (one in Koraput, two each in Malkangiri and Rayagada, one in Kalahandi), thereby making healthcare facilities available in all 80 blocks of the KBK region. The Commission noted with concern a lack of available doctors in Balangir, Malkangiri and Sonepur and directed the state-level monitoring committee to review the situation and ensure that vacancies of medical officers do not go beyond 20% of their sanctioned strength in the KBK districts.

The Commission noted with concern that though deaths due to diarrhoea seem to have been controlled in Koraput, Rayagada, Malkangiri, Nabarangpur and Sonepur, they were still continuing in Kalahandi, Nuapada and Balangir.

Regarding the menace of malaria, the Commission noted that the state government did not follow the directions given on 22 March 2000 to assess whether the existing anti-malaria measures were truly effective and to use a better strategy for tackling the disease. The Commission, therefore, called for a detailed report from the state government on this account and observed that by equipping mobile health units with testing kits, as was done in Kalahandi, malaria detection could be improved.

The Commission further noted the inadequacies and gaps in the data collection system for computing Maternal Mortality Ratio (MMR), Infant Mortality Rate (IMR) and other parameters related to the health of women and children. The state health authorities were told to extend effective health cover to the population in backward pockets especially those inhabited by Bonda, Koya, Didayi and Gond tribes in Malkangiri.

iii. Social Security Programmes

The Commission acknowledged general improvement in the execution of pension schemes and Public Distribution System (PDS) in KBK districts. The efforts that the district administration of Balangir made, based on the Special Rapporteur's suggestions, were also appreciated. It was added that those efforts needed further strengthening through a system of revolving funds and the involvement of women self-help groups.

The Commission found some interruptions in Mid-Day Meal (MDM) and Supplementary Nutrition Programme (SNP) due to late arrival of stock, despite assurances by the Chief Secretary that such interruptions would not occur. Similarly, the Commission expressed its serious concern about the slow progress in arranging door-step food supply at Anganwadi centres despite a direction regarding the same issued on 22 March 2000. Besides referring to the report of the state government which showed that Sonepur, Nabarangpur and Rayagada were still not covered under the scheme, the Commission suggested that the state government should show total compliance in the Action Taken Report on this count.

Although the state government assured "the orders are under issue," it had remained silent about the directions of the Commission dated 22 March 2000 regarding the supply of dry ration to the beneficiaries of EFPs. Based on the report by the Special Rapporteur, the Commission noted that about 40 thousand families in Nabarangpur were being denied their PDS ration on the technical ground that they were living on encroached land in the forest. The Commission directed the Chief Secretary to take care of this matter and reconsider the state government's stand that "No human habitation in reserve forest has been declared as a forest village. Unless they are declared as forest villages, and the families surveyed by the Panchayati Raj Department, PDS cannot be extended." The state government was asked to think of a feasible solution to extend the benefits of PDS to these people.

iv. Soil Conservation Programme

The Commission noted some improvement in the execution of watershed projects under EAS and NWDPRA. However, serious deficiencies and irregularities were also found in Nuapada and Sonepur. Keeping in mind the Special Rapporteur's report on this aspect and the Commission's observations made earlier, the state-level monitoring committee was directed to take necessary steps to speed up and improve the execution of watershed projects in the KBK districts, and also to curb misutilization and wastage of funds due to staff inaction or negligence. The Chief Secretary of the state assured the Commission that the watershed projects—both departmental under National Watershed Development Project for Rainfed Areas (NWDPRA) and non-departmental under Employment Assurance Scheme (EAS)—would be applied with community participation adhering to the guidelines laid down by the Ministry of Rural Affairs and Employment (MORAE) and will also be supervised by the Director of the Watershed Mission. So, the Commission expected that an ATR from the state government would give a detailed account of the execution of watershed projects.

v. Rural Development

As noted by the Commission from the overall assessment spanning January, 1998 to March 2000, schemes such as the Jawahar Rozgar Yojna (JRY) and Employment Assurance Scheme (EAS) were executed well in Koraput, Kalahandi, Rayagada, and Balangir. In Nabarangpur and Malkangiri 60-70% funds were utilized. However, Nuapada did not fare well in JRY and EAS, and Sonepur's performance in JRY was unsatisfactory.

The Commission found that the practice of quarterly allocation of targets and performance evaluation should continue in the future and that monitoring can help ensure progressive utilization of funds and efficient execution of projects. This also averted the expenditure rush towards the end of the financial year. The Commission entrusted this responsibility to the state-level monitoring committee.

vi. Land Reforms

The Commission was glad that the amendments were finalized to the Orissa Scheduled Areas Transfer of Immovable Property (by Scheduled Tribes) Regulation, 1956. This now imposed a total ban on transfer of tribal land to non-tribals, involvement of Panchayat Raj Institutions for detection of illegal land transfers and restoration of land to original owners and enforcement of the punishment for unlawful occupation of tribal land. The amendments were at the time awaiting the President's assent.[16] The Commission also noted the government's statement that necessary steps were being taken to make similar amendments to the Odisha Land Reforms Act, 1960 to prohibit transfer of land from scheduled castes to non scheduled castes.[17]

The Commission appreciated the constitution of a Task Force in the Revenue Department and the instructions to District Magistrates to detect cases of land alienation and to restore possession of such lands to the original owners. However, the Commission noted with regret that 'detection is poor, disposal of cases is poorer and restoration of land to the original owners is negligible.' This situation had been reported by the Expert Committee on Land Reforms and confirmed by the Special Rapporteur. The Commission advised the state level monitoring committee to give its utmost attention to the implementation of the existing provisions of the Land Reforms Act and to expedite government decisions on other recommendations of the expert committee relating to tenancy, separation of holdings and correction of RORs, ceiling surplus land, procurement policy (there should be no procurement target in KBK districts, as per the expert committee's recommendation), institutional credit, etc.

vii. Afforestation

The Commission appreciated the afforestation progra-mmes under block plantation, Rehabilitation of Degraded Forests (RDF) and Non-Timber Forest Products (NTFP) that were being conducted with full community support. In addition to the monitoring performed by the Forest Department, the Commission suggested another layer of monitoring by the state-level monitoring committee at regular intervals, keeping in mind the hefty amount of money involved, the gravity of the problems in KBK and towards offering long term solutions. The Commission welcomed Odisha's new NTFP policy which transferred ownership of 60 NTFP to Gram Panchayats. The Commission expressed its view that the new policy needed to be watched carefully during implementation to secure the tribal population's rights to procure, gather, use and sell non-timber forest produce.

viii. Monitoring

Consistent with its observations made on 17 February 1998, the Commission again stressed the importance of proper monitoring in effectively applying any programmes, regardless of how well-conceived they are. Monitoring was noted as being a key to improve efficiency, transparency and accountability. The Commission requested the Government of Odisha to constitute a state-level monitoring committee, headed by the chief secretary who would actually help bolster the overall efforts. The Commission regretted that the existing monitoring committee was neither meeting regularly nor making the Commission aware of its deliberations. It was also added that the initial two years fixed for short-term immediate relief measures were over and that now there was a need for long-term measures focused on offering a permanent solution to the problems of KBK. So, the Commission felt that the state-level monitoring committee should have meetings at least once every three months—to review the progress of different relief and development programmes and to direct the districts whenever necessary. The Commission asked for the future minutes of the committee along with the inspection/monitoring reports from the secretaries in-charge of the KBK districts and other concerned senior officers from Rural Water Supply & Sanitation (RWSS), Health, Soil Conservation, Women and Child Development, Panchayati Raj, Revenue and Forest etc,.

ix. Literacy and Education

The Commission saw that the literacy level (1990-91 census) of KBK region was 29.24% against the Odisha state average of 49.1%. The literacy level of KBK's scheduled tribes population was said to be 13.1% with female literacy as low as 3.89%. Overall education level, especially primary education, was very disappointing in tribal pockets; enrollments were low, absentee rate was high and the percentage of dropouts large. There was also a general shortage of science and mathematics teachers in high schools leading to poor results. So, the Commission expected the state government to formulate policies and launch programmes that would actually improve the quality and extent of the educational facilities in the state. Further, the Commission reiterated its directions given on 3 November 1998 and asked the state government to identify some credible NGOs and involve them in raising awareness about literacy programmes. The Commission expected that an ATR should contain the said aspect and also results achieved.

Deficiencies and Shortfalls: Report of the Special Rapporteur

(Hearing held on 10.10.2002[18])

Chaman Lal, Special Rapporteur, after visiting the KBK districts submitted his report which reflected both—progress and deficiency.

The Commission also pondered on the nature and character of the human rights involved in the case and if it needed to be addressed. Further, on hearing the state government's assurance that it would file a detailed response to the observations made by different parties, the Commission felt that it was necessary to organize a joint meeting between the counsel/representatives appearing for various parties, the Chief Secretary and other concerned officers of government of Odisha, along with the Special Rapporteur. The purpose of the meeting was to build consensus on maximum issues.

Chaman Lal, Special Rapporteur, in his presentation made before the Commission on 10 October, 2002, summed up the progress made on different issues as follows:

i. Rural Water Supply and Sanitation

The Self-Employed Mechanics (SEMs) scheme had been fully introduced in Koraput, Nuapada, Malkangiri and Nabarangpur. The assurance of its full implementation in Rayagada and Balangir was to be confirmed by the Government of Odisha. The scheme was not adequately carried out in Kalahandi where only five blocks out of total thirteen had been covered, and in Sonepur, where the scheme was not introduced in any block till February, 2002 when the compliance report was sent.

The Special Rapporteur had, in his visit note, pointed out the poor maintenance of hand-pumps in Balangir and Sonepur and said that the compliance report gave no satisfactory response except saying that SEM would be introduced. He also recognized the need for testing the quality of water in pockets of high iron content as was directed by the Commission proceedings of 9 June, 1999.

ii. Primary Health Care

During its proceedings held on 14 December, 2000, the Commission had directed that vacancies of medical officers in KBK districts should never be allowed to exceed 20% of the sanctioned strength. This direction was followed only in Koraput (16%), Balangir (7%) and Sonepur (22%). Vacancies of medical officers in other districts were disheartening.

Malkangiri	39.5%
Nabarangpur	36%
Rayagada	28%
Kalahandi	40%
Nuapada	29%

Vacancies of para-medical staff (nurse, pharmacists and lab technicians) remained unfilled in most districts. There also was a need to ration the postings of available specialists in every KBK district.

There were irregularities in food supply to indoor patients in government hospitals at most places. The Special Rapporteur suggested setting up of additional sub-centres in Koraput and Nabarangpur and for assessing similar needs of other districts. There was also a need for a special MHU for block Kasargunda (dist. Nabarangpur) to cover nine GPs that remained cut off for nine months a year.

iii. Social Security

Interruptions in the Supplementary Nutrition Programme (SNP) occurred due to diversion of World Food Programme supplies to flood-affected areas. Corn Soya Blend (CSB) was to be substituted by India-mix, and it was well ensured in Malkangiri, but interruptions were found in Koraput and Nabarangpur. Some delays were marked in the introduction of door-step supply under the Mid-Day Meal programme in Sonepur district (introduced on 1 April, 2002), Rayagada (on 20 March 2002) and Nabarangpur (on 20 April, 2002).

The Mid-Day Meal scheme was poorly covered (81% in 1999, 66% in 1999-2000 and 57% in 2000-01). The government, in response, assured the Commission that with the transfer of this subject from the Civil Supply Department to the Women and Child Department, the desired improvement had taken place. The Commission expected that district-wise data of 2001-2002 and up to 30 September 2002 would be furnished to support the claim.

There was a need to extend the PDS facility to 1857 forest-dwelling families of Nabarangpur. GPs also needed to be involved. PDS in Kalahandi had involved only 14 GPs out of total 195 so far.

Some gaps were detected in the Emergency Feeding Programme in Kalahandi where beneficiaries were given 3.8 kg rice for 23 days a month instead of 5 kg for 30 days. District-wise number of beneficiaries in schemes of Antyodaya and Annapurna—as of 30 September 2002—was to be provided, to support the claim that allotted targets have all been met.

iv. Soil Conservation

There was a need for sample evaluation of completed projects under NWDPRA vis-à-vis achievement claimed. Twenty NWDPRA projects were taken up under the Ninth Plan in Nabarangpur, ten of which were discontinued following instructions from the Director, Soil Conservation, obviously after incurring some initial expenditure. The Department needed to provide an explanation.

Decisions regarding reorientation of NWDPRA projects to the MORAE guidelines were not implemented in most districts. The compliance report was silent on this point. 30 watershed development projects under the EAS were dropped in Koraput, 31 in Nabarangpur and 9 in Sonepur after incurring expenditure on initial activities including community mobilization and training. This again needed explanation. Progress of projects under EAS in every district was nevertheless commended by the Special Rapporteur.

v. Rural Development

JGSY: As of February 2002, performance was poor in Malkangiri (48% financial and 58% physical), Balangir (51% financial and 55% physical).

EAS: As of February 2002, performance mentioned in the compliance report was poor in Malkangiri (30% financial and 65% physical), Rayagada (40% financial and 76% physical), Balangir (49% financial and 52% physical), Nuapada (31% financial and 64% physical) and Sonepur (49% financial and 102% physical).

SJGSY : All the districts appeared to be doing well. The state monitoring committee, however, was not meeting quarterly as directed by the Commission as far back as 17 February 1998 and as reiterated from time to time.

vi. Afforestation

LTAP was being executed smoothly in all districts. The level of community mobilization was commendable. Targets were gradually being achieved under all heads and the survival rate was fine. However, all districts were facing some constraints.

- Delays in release of funds were affecting the schedule of new plantations and maintenance jobs like weeding, application of insecticides, fertilizers and soil conservation measures.
- Inadequate, untimely supply of food-grains under the World Food Programme, which started in 1999. The supply of food packets was a powerful incentive. Food availability varied from district to district, ranging from 30% to 70% of the total requirement.
- Implementation of NTFP had empowered the GPs to regulate procurement and trading of 68 items. Minimum support price (MSP) fixed by the Collectors was not being enforced uniformly.
- GPs should be made stakeholders by extending some financial incentives (Special Rapporteur had recommended 1% of the sale proceeds). Legislative measures through amending acts and rules related to NTFP were expected.

vii. Land Reforms

In proceedings on 22 March 2000, the Commission had asked the Government of Odisha to intimate the proposed follow-up on the recommendations of the land-reforms committee. The amendment of Regulation 2/56 had finally come through (as informed by the Revenue Secretary during the course of the hearing). The government was now required to take up the promised measure of bringing about similar amendments in the Orissa Land Reforms Act to ban transfer of land from SCs to non-SCs.

There was a lack of proper adherence to the instructions issued by the Revenue Department to District Collectors for a continuous drive to detect cases of land alienation and unauthorized possession, to prosecute the offenders and restore land to their rightful owners. District-wise monitoring needed to be strengthened. The Special Rapporteur had commended Koraput, Rayagada and Balangir but found the results in Malkangiri, Sonepur and Nuapada poor.

viii. Distress sale of paddy in all districts

The Special Rapporteur had discussed this in the state-level meeting and noted the suggestions made by the Collector, Subarnapur. The government, in its response, had acknowledged the need for increasing storage space for FCI, purchase of paddy by the FCI, direct purchase from farmers and stoppage of paddy procurement transactions outside the mandis. Rural indebtedness was considered a major cause of distress sale.

Emphasis on the Long-Term, and more ideas on the Right to Food

(Hearing held on 17.01.2003[19])

On this hearing, the Commission referred to the orders dated 28 April, 1997 and 26 July 1997 passed by the Hon'ble Supreme Court in W.P.(C) No.42/97 filed by Indian Council of Legal Aid and Advice and Ors., and noted that as per the NHRC Report of 2 January, 1997—based on its visit to KBK districts between 12-17 December, 1996:

> ...because of the very high level of deprivation existing in the area, along with extensive crop damage, malnourishment, inadequate income levels and insufficient outreach of relief measures, the possibility of deaths having occurred owing to prolonged malnutrition and hunger, compounded by diseases, could not be ruled out. Indeed out of 21 deates investigated, 17 were attributable to such causes.

The Commission summed up progress reported during the eleven hearings that had taken place before it between 3 September, 1997 and 29 January, 1998. During these proceedings, the Commission had examined, *inter-alia*, economic theories on starvation and famine, the socio-economic and environmental background of Odisha (and especially KBK districts) over the past decade, how the state government and Centre responded to situations prevailing in the KBK districts, and possible 2 years' interim measures, meant to be dove-tailed into a long term plan to permanently end the deprivation, malnutrition and cyclical starvation in the KBK districts.

The Commission then proceeded to discuss the proposed long term measures.

i) Revised Long Term Action Plan (RLTAP)

The Commission noted that the Government of Odisha had originally launched a seven-year Long Term Action Plan (LTAP) applicable to the years from 1995-96 to 2001-02. However, a Revised Long Term Action Plan (RLTAP) for the KBK districts was created on advice of the Government of India in 1998 covering seven years from 1998-99 to 2006-07. The RLTAP had primarily three objectives, i.e., drought proofing, development saturation and poverty alleviation and also improvement in the quality of life of the local people. RLTAP was focused on the issues of agriculture, horticulture, watershed development, afforestation, irrigation, health, drinking water emergency feeding, welfare of SCs/STs and rural connectivity sectors. The total financial outlay was Rs.6251.08 crore including normal flow of plan funds under Central Plan (CP) and Centrally Sponsored Plan (CSP) schemes and also additional/special funds to be received from the Government of India. The Commission noted that the Government of Odisha had set up a Special Area Development Project, KBK, headquartered at Koraput, with a senior officer designated as Chief Administrator to supervise and monitor the implementation of RLTAP. Also, a Project Level Committee (PLC) under the Chairmanship of the Chief Secretary, and a State Level Committee (SLC) under the Chairmanship of the Chief Minister were formed for the same purpose.

ii. Monitoring

The Commission also considered the question of monitoring and hoped that the state-level monitoring committee would meet at least once in every three months to keep an eye on the works of the various departments.

Also, the Commission agreed with the petitioners counsel that the Special Area KBK project should have District-Level Committees (DLC), to look after the execution of programmes as allotted by the Chief Administrator. In addition, the petitioners wanted the Performance Appraisal Reports of the districts to be made public; and the Chief Administrator to hold public hearings every six months in each of the KBK districts in rotation during which salient features of all developmental programmes along with the information about the achievement of physical and financial targets would be shared with the public at district and block levels. Information should reach the public through booklets and handouts from time to time. The Commission agreed with these suggestions. The state government, in turn, agreed to set up the DLCs.

Moreover, the Commission also endorsed the recommendations made in the 106th report of the Rajya Sabha Committee regarding periodical review of execution of the RLTAP by a Committee of Secretaries to the government of India under the Chairmanship of the Cabinet Secretary. Further, the Commission observed the general consensus among the parties about the continuous involvement of the NHRC in overall monitoring of the programmes. The Commission felt that associating the Special Rapporteur of the Commission with the quarterly meetings of the state-level committee and his continued visits to the selected districts of KBK region would serve the purpose. The Commission acknowledged and forwarded requests made by the Government of Odisha through its counsel that:

(i) The RLTAP should be made an integral part of the 10th Plan document and should be formally approved in all respects; and
(ii) Year-wise availability of funds should be indicated for the entire 10th Plan period and funds should be released well in advance in order to obviate the ad-hoc nature of the current arrangement.

iii. Special Category Status

The State of Odisha sought the NHRC's intervention to expedite its proposal to the Government of India to declare the State of Odisha as a special category state in view of poverty, chronic backwardness, weak tax base and the serious debt trap it faced. The Commission was informed that the proposal was under consideration of the Government of India. Considering the state's request, the Commission agreed to recommend at least KBK region of Odisha for special category status, if not Odisha as a whole, owing to the ceaseless hunger, poverty and unemployment affecting much of its population.

iv. The Right to Food

The Commission considered the Right to Food as a part of Art. 21 of the Constitution:

> Article 21 of the Constitution of India guarantees a fundamental right to life and personal liberty. The expression 'Life' in this Article has been judicially interpreted to mean a life with human dignity and not mere survival or animal existence. In the light of this the State is obliged to provide for all those minimum requirements which must be satisfied in order to enable a person to live with human dignity, such as education, health care, just and humane conditions of work protection against exploitation etc. In the view of the Commission the Right to Food is inherent to a life with dignity, and Article 21 should be read with Articles 39(a) of the Constitution, enunciated as one of the Directive Principles, fundamental in the governance of the country, requires the State to direct its policy towards securing that the livelihood. Article 47 spells out the duty of the State to raise the level of nutrition and the standard of living of its people as a primary responsibility. The citizen's right to be free from hunger enshrined in Article 21 is to be ensured by the fulfillment of the obligations of the State set out in Articles 39(a) and 47. The reading of Article 21 together with Articles 39(a) and 47, places, the issue of food security in the correct perspective, thus making the Right to Food a guaranteed Fundamental Right which is enforceable by virtue of the constitutional remedy provided under Article 32 of the Constitution. The requirements of the Constitution preceded, and are consonant with, the obligations of the State under the 1966 international Covenant of the Economic, Social and Cultural Rights to which India is a party. That Covenant, in Article 11, expressly recognises the right of everyone to an adequate standard of living, including adequate food.

The Commission recognized that the deaths of people suffering from prolonged hunger and deprivation in the KBK districts, may not always be regarded as "starvation deaths" in the strict clinical sense of the term, but it was undeniable that extreme hunger and malnourishment had weakened them so much, that they were unable to fight or recover from infirmities or common diseases like malaria or diarrhoea. What was more shocking is that this situation continued when the granaries of the Food Corporation of India (FCI) were overflowing. The Commission held that the existing practice of relying on mortality as a proof of starvation is wrong and needs to be set aside.

Further, the Commission acknowledged that availing oneself of the right to food is nothing without meeting appropriate nutritional levels, and that the quantum of relief to those in distress must meet those levels. Failing to make this happen, keeps the right to food as a mere theoretical concept. A need for a paradigm shift in public policies and the relief codes regarding the same was also felt. On this basis, amendment of paragraphs 163, 164, 168(b) and 169 of the Orissa Relief Code was sought to bring the code in line with the Constitution of India. This needed to be done to accomplish the following:

(a) A paradigm shift from the domain of benevolence to that of right.
(b) A change from the assessment of harvest to the assessment of hunger.
(c) A shift in timing of state intervention to the hunger season; and,
(d) A devising of the terms of cognizance for starvation and destitution.

The state replied that a committee has been formed headed by the Agricultural Production Commissioner (APC) and other officers as well as non-official members to deliberate on the above suggestions on amendments in the Orissa Relief Code.

Dr. Rangasami, one of the petitioners, suggested the following for consideration of the Centre:

(a) The need to revise the present criteria used to determine 'relief'. The 'basket' of relief provided should be prescribed in terms of adequate nutritional requirements and not in fixed monetary terms. This would automatically revise the outlays required to keep pace with rising costs.
(b) The devising of the criteria for the provision of assistance to small farmers in a manner which links it to the elimination of destitution and the halting of distress migration, distress sale of crops, labour and land and protection against impoverishment.

The Commission could see how valuable these questions were regarding the quantum of resources required for calamity relief and the method of their utilization.

Dr. Rangasami was requested to develop the ideas further and provide the Commission with a paper on the subject, so that, Government of India's views can be obtained.

The Commission also made the following significant observation:

> In concluding these Proceedings, the Commission would like to observe that they are being held at a time when, universally, there is a demand that every effort be made by the State and by civil society to eradicate the poverty and hunger that constitute an affront to the dignity and worth of the human person. First and foremost among the United Nations Millennium Development Goals (MDG) is the pledge made by all Heads of State and Government to halve, by the year 2015, the proportion of the world's poor and of people who suffer from hunger. Given the circumstances of our country. India has a special responsibility in their regard. The prevalence of extreme poverty and hunger is unconscionable in this day and age, for not only does it militate against respect for human rights, but it also undermines the prospects of peace and harmony within a State. For all of these reasons, the Commission will continue to be deeply involved with the issues raised in these hearings in the period ahead.

Examination of the Compliance Report

(Hearing held on 8.10.2003[20])

The Government of Odisha through its communication dated 17 July 2003 submitted a compliance report with regard to the various recommendations of the Commission. The Commission asked the Special Rapporteur to examine it. The special Rapporteur drew the attention of the Commission to the following issues:

a) The report on the amendment of the Odisha Relief Code, for which a Committee headed by the Agriculture Production Commissioner (APC) was formed by the Odisha government in December, 2002, had not been received so far;

b) The Odisha government should also convey to the Commission the progress on the implementation of the Long-Term Action Plan based on the monitoring carried out by it.

The Commission directed compliance of the above points by the state government.

Status Report

(Hearing held on 08.04.2004[21])

The Commission asked the State of Odisha to file the up-to-date status report (till 31 March 2004) both with regard to Short Term and Long Term measures and steps in the pipe-line for meeting the situation, with an advance copy to be given to the counsel for the petitioners. It is directed that the copies of the status report from the State of Odisha as well as the comments of Shri Sanjay Parikh (petitioners' counsel) would be passed on to Shri Chaman Lal, Special Rapporteur, who was requested to visit the KBK districts for an on-the-spot verification followed by his report.

HEARINGS BY CHIEF JUSTICE (RETD) A.S. ANAND :

After Justice Verma's tenure was over, Justice A.S. Anand, Chief Justice (Retd.) of the Supreme Court, took over the proceedings, to complete the unfinished task.

A final task for the Special Rapporteur

(Hearing held on 28.07.2005[22])

In this hearing, the Commission took cognizance of the quarterly performance appraisal reports sent by the Government of Odisha since January, 1999, scrutinized and physically verified by the Special Rapporteur. The Commission noted that the government of Odisha had submitted two reports dated 30 June, 2004 and 19 November 2004 to show the status of the compliance by the state government (till March, 2004). On these reports, counsel for the petitioners had made various observations. The state government responded to those observations and furnished a compilation of supporting documents. The Special Rapporteur-Chaman Lal was asked to visit the KBK districts for verifying on ground the execution of long term and short term plans. He was requested to submit his report on all essential areas with which the Commission was concerned. In these proceedings, the NHRC also directed that the state level committee headed by the Chief Secretary should meet periodically and evaluate the action taken on the short term and long term plans.

Special Rapporteur's Report on Compliance

Following the above proceedings dated 28 July 2005, Special Rapporteur-Chaman Lal visited the KBK districts from 11 to 23 December, 2005 and submitted his comments district-wise on all issues. The changes that had taken place in crucial areas, namely, drinking water, primary health and social security in all the eight districts are mentioned below:

<table>
<tr><th>Category</th><th>Observations by the Special Rapporteur</th></tr>
<tr><td colspan="2">KORAPUT</td></tr>
<tr><td>Drinking water</td><td>The scheme regarding self-employed mechanics (SEM) for repairing defunct tube wells was in operation in all 14 blocks. No complaints were received on drinking water supply during the field visit. The target of one spot source per 250 population, directed by the NHRC as an interim measure, was fully achieved before 31 March 2001. On revision of scale, i.e., one spot source for 150 population, the drinking water supply improved further as follows:
<table>
<tr><th>Spot Source</th><th>As of 1.4.01</th><th>As of 1.4.05</th><th>As of 30.11.05</th></tr>
<tr><td>Tube well</td><td>6550</td><td>8518</td><td>8705</td></tr>
<tr><td>Sanitary well</td><td>648</td><td>1233</td><td>1249</td></tr>
<tr><td>Spring based</td><td>72</td><td>128</td><td>128</td></tr>
<tr><td>Total:</td><td>7270</td><td>7879</td><td>1082</td></tr>
</table>
</td></tr>
<tr><td>Primary health care</td><td>63 health institutions including 5 PHCs and 47 PHCs (M). Vacancy of doctors reduced to 13% only. 15 Mobile Health Units (MHU) became operational. The field visit of the MHUs was extended from 20 (previous) to 28 days in a month, to cover remote/all approachable villages. Each MHU was allowed two-night halts per month. There was some success in the reduction of deaths due to malaria and diarrhoea, displayed as follows:
<table>
<tr><th>Year</th><th>Deaths due to diarrhoea</th><th>Deaths due to malaria</th></tr>
<tr><td>2001</td><td></td><td>29</td></tr>
<tr><td>2002</td><td>47</td><td>26</td></tr>
<tr><td>2003</td><td>37</td><td>41</td></tr>
<tr><td>2004</td><td>34</td><td>25</td></tr>
<tr><td>2005</td><td>21</td><td>18</td></tr>
</table>
This aspect needs continous attention and efforts.</td></tr>
</table>

<table>
<tr><td>Social security</td><td>The target under the National Old Age Pension (NOAP) was enhanced from 17055 to 46782 in October, 2001 and was achieved 100% every year since then. Similarly, targets of State Old Age Pension (SOAP) and ODB were raised from 2280 to 23960 and from 3783 to 4439 respectively after last review and were achieved 100%.
Emergency feeding program expanded from three blocks, to all 14 blocks. Target was increased from 7600 to 37350 beneficiaries in 2001 and there was a 100% achievement of the target.
Supplementary nutrition programmes for children, pregnant and lactating mothers as well as Integrated Child Development Services (ICDS) were also achieved.
All 14 blocks were covered under the targeted Public Distribution Scheme.</td></tr>
<tr><td colspan="2">RAYAGADA</td></tr>
<tr><td>Drinking water</td><td>The target of one spot source for 250 population taken up for monitoring by the NHRC was realized well before 1 April, 2001. Following the revision of scale to one spot source for 150 population, the number had been increasing in the district every year as depicted below:
<table>
<tr><th>Spot Source</th><th>As of 1.4.01</th><th>As of 1.4.05</th><th>As of 1.11.05</th></tr>
<tr><td>Tube well</td><td>6054</td><td>7360</td><td>7583</td></tr>
<tr><td>Sanitary well</td><td>345</td><td>866</td><td>949</td></tr>
<tr><td>Spring based</td><td>18</td><td>34</td><td>36</td></tr>
<tr><td>Piped supply</td><td>18</td><td>37</td><td>45</td></tr>
<tr><td>Total:</td><td>6435</td><td>8297</td><td>8613</td></tr>
</table>
The Self-Employed Mechanic Scheme was working in all the blocks. A total of 310 SEMs were posted after proper training.</td></tr>
<tr><td>Primary health care</td><td>There were 49 medical institutions including 5 CHC, 6 PHC and 34 PHC (new). 5 PHCs, which had been sanctioned, were not made functional. MHUs increased from 4 in 1995-96 to 12, one in each block and one extra in Kashipur block to give access to interior pockets of the district.</td></tr>
<tr><td>Social security</td><td>The target under NOAP was increased from 1106 to 25259 on 1 April, 2002. The number of beneficiaries under SOAP increased from 16113 to 18913. The target of ODP was enhanced from 2279 to 3081 in 2002-03 and further raised to 3689 in 2004-05.</td></tr>
</table>

<table>
<tr><td></td><td>EFP was extended from 3 blocks and 6000 beneficiaries to 11 blocks and 22840, along with permission to supply dry ration to beneficiaries in 3 blocks who find it difficult to walk to the centre for daily meals. The number of beneficiaries receiving dry ration was 1012 in Kashipur, 367 in Ramaguda and 289 in Chanderpur.</td></tr>
<tr><td colspan="2">MALKANGIRI</td></tr>
<tr><td>Drinking water

1.4.01</td><td>The target of one spot source for 250 population was achieved well before 31 March 2001. The target was thereafter revised to 150.
The status of spot source was as follows:
<table>
<tr><th>Spot Source
1.4.05</th><th>As of
31.11.05</th><th>As of</th><th>As of</th></tr>
<tr><td>Tube well</td><td>3727</td><td>4701</td><td>4815</td></tr>
<tr><td>Sanitary well</td><td>357</td><td>556</td><td>556</td></tr>
<tr><td>Spring based</td><td>5</td><td>5</td><td>5</td></tr>
<tr><td>Piped supply</td><td>4</td><td>24</td><td>24</td></tr>
<tr><td>Total:</td><td>4093</td><td>5286</td><td>4900</td></tr>
</table>
The SEM scheme was in operation in all blocks. Out of 182 deployed SEMs, only 162 were available as of 30.11.05.</td></tr>
<tr><td>Primary health care</td><td>There were 38 health institutions including 3 CHC, 3 PHC and 25 PHC (new). 6 PHC (new) were non-functional. 10 MHUs were providing medical cover to remote villages. They toured for 20 days a month and made 5 night halts.</td></tr>
<tr><td>Social security</td><td>Pension schemes such as NOAP, SOAP and ODP were running smoothly. The target under NOAP had been increased from 7054 to 16528. The number of beneficiaries increased from 1170 in 2002-03 to 1360 in 2004-05 and further to 1469 in 2005-06. The number of beneficiaries under SOAP went up from 11832 to 12332. All these targets were being achieved fully. Emergency feeding was increased from 4 blocks and 8200 beneficiaries to all 7 blocks and 14990 beneficiaries.</td></tr>
<tr><td colspan="2">NABARANGPUR</td></tr>
<tr><td>Drinking water</td><td>The target of one spot source for 250 population was achieved well before 31 March 2001. The target was thereafter revised to 150.
The status of spot source was as follows:</td></tr>
</table>

<table>
<tr><td></td><td><table><tr><th>Spot Source</th><th>As of 1.4.01</th><th>As of 1.4.05</th><th>As of 31.11.05</th></tr><tr><td>Tube well</td><td>6001</td><td>8301</td><td>8739</td></tr><tr><td>Sanitary well</td><td>115</td><td>202</td><td>215</td></tr><tr><td>Piped supply</td><td>13</td><td>30</td><td>31</td></tr><tr><td>Total:</td><td>6129</td><td>8532</td><td>8985</td></tr></table>The SEM scheme was in operation in all blocks, with 292 trained SEMs employed in 10 blocks.</td></tr>
<tr><td>Primary health care</td><td>There were 50 health institutions including 7 CHC, 3 PHC and 37 PHC (N). 4 sanctioned PHCs were not operational. 11 mobile health units were touring for 24 days in a month.</td></tr>
<tr><td>Social security</td><td>The number of beneficiaries under NOAP increased from 14092 to 29729, under SOAP from 20619 to 21619, and under ODP from 3043 to 3695. Emergency feeding programme, introduced in 2001 with a target of 19270, was being fully utilized.</td></tr>
<tr><td colspan="2">KALAHANDI</td></tr>
<tr><td>Drinking water</td><td>The target of one spot source for 250 population was achieved well before 31.03.01. The target was thereafter revised to 150.

The status of spot source was as follows:<table><tr><th>Spot Source</th><th>As of 1.4.01</th><th>As of 1.4.05</th><th>As of 30.11.05</th></tr><tr><td>Tube well</td><td>8656</td><td>11962</td><td>11962</td></tr><tr><td>Sanitary well</td><td>108</td><td>227</td><td>243</td></tr><tr><td>Total:</td><td>8764</td><td>12189</td><td>12205</td></tr></table>The SEM scheme was in operation in all blocks, with 389 SEMs in 13 blocks.</td></tr>
<tr><td>Primary health care</td><td>The district has a total of 65 health institutions including 10 UPHC/CHG, 4 PHC and 29 PHC (new). 14 mobile health institutions were in place in the district. Until Oct 2005, 1987 tours had been taken in the year to cover 2111 villages and 1,84,708 patients.</td></tr>
<tr><td>Social security</td><td>NOAP, SOAP and ODP were functioning smoothly. The target under NOAP has increased from 18825 in 2001 to 22825, under SOAP from 42914 to 44214 and under ODP from 4601 to 5555. The target under EFP was increased from 22245 to 37200 in 2001-02. The district was running 1214 feeding centres.</td></tr>
</table>

<table>
<tr><th colspan="2">NUAPADA</th></tr>
<tr><td>Drinking water</td><td>The target of one spot source for 250 population was achieved well before 31 March 2001. The target was thereafter revised to 150.
The status of spot source was as follows:
<table>
<tr><th>Spot Source</th><th>As of 1.4.01</th><th>As of 1.4.05</th><th>As of 30.11.05</th></tr>
<tr><td>Tube well</td><td>4328</td><td>5739</td><td>5748</td></tr>
<tr><td>Sanitary well</td><td>7</td><td>55</td><td>62</td></tr>
<tr><td>Total:</td><td>4335</td><td>5794</td><td>5810</td></tr>
</table>
The SEM scheme had been introduced in all the blocks with deployment of 199 SEMs.</td></tr>
<tr><td>Primary health care</td><td>Nuapada had 22 health institutions-1 District Hospital, 3 CHC, 1 UG PHC, 2 PHC and 15 PHC (N). 7 MHUs were functioning but managed by Ayurvedic doctors, with a monthly tour of 24 days.</td></tr>
<tr><td>Social security</td><td>The target under NOAP was increased from 11118 to 19750 in 2002-03. Quota of SOAP was increased from 13410 to 15019 in 2003-04 and again to 15519 in 2004-05. The target under ODP was increased from 1590 to 2264 in 2003-04 and further to 2398 in 2005-06. The target under EFP was increased from 13000 to 21000 in 2001-02, which was being fully utilized. 12550 persons were shown in the waiting list.</td></tr>
<tr><th colspan="2">BALANGIR</th></tr>
<tr><td>Drinking water</td><td>The target of one spot source for 250 population was achieved well before 31 March 01. The target was thereafter revised to 150.
The status of spot source was as follows:
<table>
<tr><th>Spot Source</th><th>As of 1.4.01</th><th>As of 1.4.05</th><th>As of 30.11.05</th></tr>
<tr><td>Tube well</td><td>8793</td><td>11514</td><td>11687</td></tr>
<tr><td>Sanitary well</td><td>3</td><td>3</td><td>3</td></tr>
<tr><td>Piped supply</td><td>36</td><td>68</td><td>71</td></tr>
<tr><td>Total:</td><td>8832</td><td>11585</td><td>11761</td></tr>
</table>
The SEM scheme had been introduced in all the blocks with deployment of 459 SEMs.</td></tr>
<tr><td>Primary health care</td><td>Balangir had 59 health institutions including 9 PHCs and 38 PHCs (new).</td></tr>
</table>

<table>
<tr><td>Social security</td><td>The number of beneficiaries under NOAP was increased from 28978 to 39313 in 2002-03. The number of beneficiaries under SOAP was increased from 22022 to 24522 in 2003-04 and 25822 in 2004-05. Number of beneficiaries under ODP was increased from 4111 in 2001-03 to 5342 in 2003-04, 5796 in 2004-05, and to 6089 in 2005-06. The number of beneficiaries under the EFP was increased from 20,000 to 33,860 in 2001-02.</td></tr>
<tr><td colspan="2">SUBARNAPUR</td></tr>
<tr><td>Drinking water</td><td>The target of one spot source for 250 population was achieved well before 31.03.01. The target was thereafter revised to 150. The status of spot source was as follows:
<table>
<tr><th>Spot Source</th><th>As of 1.4.01</th><th>As of 1.4.05</th><th>As of 30.11.05</th></tr>
<tr><td>Tube well</td><td>3535</td><td>4899</td><td>4939</td></tr>
</table>
The SEM scheme had been introduced in all the blocks with deployment of 459 SEMs.</td></tr>
<tr><td>Primary health care</td><td>Subranpur (Sonepur) had 26 health institutions including 1 PHC and 17 PHC (New). 7 Mobile Health Units were functioning in this district and their visits were increased from 20 to 24 days in a month.</td></tr>
<tr><td>Social security</td><td>The target under NOAP was increased from 7956 to 16798 in 2001. The target under SOAP was increased from 8697 to 9197 in 2004. The target under ODP was increased from 1227 to 1707 in 2003-04 and to 2071 from 01.04.2005, and further to 2202 in 2005-06. The target under EFP was revised from 13525 in 2001-02 to 18941 in 2003-04 by the Special Relief Commissioner. However, due to a shortfall in funds, this additional target was not given effect to.</td></tr>
</table>

Final proceeding: Achievements summarized

(Hearing held on 30.08.2006[23])

This was the last hearing during which the NHRC finally assessed the changes which took place in the KBK districts of State of Odisha, after considering the elaborate report of the Special Rapporteur, submissions by counsel for the petitioners (Sanjay Parikh) and the State of Odisha.

The proceedings first recalled the background which led to the initiation of the case. The Commission observed that the expression 'right to life' contained in Article 21 of the Constitution of India has been judicially interpreted to mean not only a life of survival or animal existence, but a "life with human dignity". Hence, the State was obliged to provide at least those minimum requirements that are essential to enable a person to live with human dignity, and the right to food, in the opinion of the Commission, was inherent to a life with dignity. The International Covenant on Economic, Social and Cultural Rights of 1966—to which India is a party—clearly recognizes, in Article 11, every person's right to an adequate standard of living, including sufficient food.

The Report of the Special Rapporteur pointed out that the BPL card holders in Odisha were receiving only 25 kg rice per family per month as against their entitlement of 35 kg because of a huge difference in the estimation of BPL families identified by the Government of India and the state government. It was clarified during the hearing by the Principal Secretary (Revenue) that the Government of India was allocating BPL rice to the states based on 1993-94 poverty estimates of the Planning Commission as on 1 March 2000—as projected by the Registrar General of India. Accordingly, allocations for Odisha had been limited to an estimated 32.98 lakh BPL households, whereas the state government had, in its door-to-door survey, identified 50.19 lakh BPL households. Due to this reason, the state government was compelled to allocate only 25 kg of rice per month to a BPL family, though the poorer category of BPL families covered by the Antyodaya Anna Yojana (AAY) were being provided 35 kg of rice a month.

The Commission requested the Government of India to appreciate the request made by the state government and suitably enhance the allocation of BPL rice @ 35 kg per month to 50.19 lakh BPL households, until the findings of the 2002 survey under the Supreme Court's scrutiny were finalized.

The Special Rapporteur also pointed out that there was a large number of pending unsettled claims under the National Family Benefit Scheme (NFBS) in every district. The Government of India had been approached by the state government to release a sum of Rs.50 crore to clear up the pending claims of 53,254 beneficiaries under NFBS in Odisha which included 12,268 belonging to the KBK districts. The Commission requested the Government of India (Women and Child Development Department) to take urgent action on this matter.

The Commission was of the view that the KBK region, being equated with the country's most backward districts, should have the funds released from the Government of India in time and also, the funds should be increased, if necessary. On no condition should they be curtailed.

The Commission appreciated the efforts of the state government to efficiently operationalize Annapurna and Antyodaya schemes under the Public Distribution System. The proposed involvement of village mothers' committees in the monitoring of SNP and EFP was commended. These committees could ensure effective monitoring of 'Take Home' foodstuff for children in the 0-3 years age group. The Commission recorded its satisfaction about steps taken for involvement of the Gram Panchayats (GPs) and village women Self Help Groups in running the PDS.

i. Soil Conservation

The observations of the Special Rapporteur regarding the execution of NWDPRA and EAS Watershed Projects were considered by the Commission and it was said that the proper execution of such works called for serious remedial action. The Commission was pleased that the suggestion regarding the evaluation of these projects had been accepted by the state government and expert bodies like ISRO (Kharagpur), IIM (Calcutta) and ISRO (Bangalore) had been engaged in the task. It was hoped that this evaluation would not only help fix accountability for the past deficiencies and irregularities, but also help check the on-going NWDPRA, IWDP and other watershed projects under the RLTAP.

ii. Rural Development Programme

While noting with satisfaction the efficient execution of various rural development schemes—such as SGSY, SGRY and IAY—the Commission found that these had not really helped much in dealing with the problem of rural unemployment. It was hoped that an efficient implementation of the newly introduced National Rural Employment Guarantee Scheme—if extended to the KBK districts—would bring about the desired change.

The Commission, therefore, recommended that allotment of targets to the districts, and performance appraisal should be made on quarterly basis, as was evolved by the Commission for the short-term measures. Besides facilitating effective monitoring, this would ensure smooth and progressive utilization of funds and avoid rush of expenditure towards the end of a financial year.

iii. Afforestation

The Commission noted with appreciation the generally satisfactory execution of the LTAP with people's participation. The Special Rapporteur had observed the reluctance of the subordinate staff to make the members of the Vana Samrakshana Samithi (VSS) aware of their ownership rights over the minor forest produce. So, it was necessary to launch a sensitization programme for the field functionaries and intensify awareness programmes for the villagers involved in these projects. The Commission appreciated the decision of the state government to assign an impact evaluation study to IIFM, Bhopal in response to the suggestion regarding the need for evaluation of the new NTMFP Policy introduced by the state government through its notification dated 31 March 2000.

iv. Land Reforms

During its proceedings of 17 January, 2003, the Commission had expressed its satisfaction about the amendment of Regulation 2 of 1956 which completely banned the transfer of land from tribals to non-tribals in scheduled areas of the state comprising 13 districts, including 8 districts of KBK. However, the report of the Special Rapporteur, after his latest field visit, showed that the follow-up action on amended provisions was not satisfactory. With a view to derive the intended benefit of these progressive measures for the welfare of the tribal population, the Commission recommended that special drives should be launched in all districts and the performance of the District Collectors evaluated accordingly. The Commission reiterated its recommendations made in its earlier proceedings of 17 January, 2003 to bring about the comprehensive suggestions made by the expert committee on land reforms. The Principal Secretary, Revenue, during the final hearing, informed the Commission about a series of measures initiated by the state government to introduce land reforms and referred to 'Mission Bhumi,' Project 'Vasundara' and the Land Passbook schemes in that connection. The measures introduced needed to be monitored properly for deriving best results.

The Commission reminded the state government about its commitment to welcome changes in tune with amendment 2/56 of the Orissa Land Reforms Act, 1960. The Principal Revenue Secretary informed the Commission that a high-level committee headed by the Chief Minister was set up to examine the relevant provisions of Regulation 2/56 in order to bring forth further amendments in order to safeguard the interest of the tribals and that after the committee's Report was received and examined, the government would process the matter so as to ban completely the transfer of tribal land to non-tribals in non-schedule areas. The Commission recommended that appropriate steps should be taken in this regard expeditiously.

Progress at a Glance

The overall progress made through the course of the proceedings (spanning over nearly nine years) was summarised as follows:

i) **Rural Water Sanitation and Supply:** The target of 'one tube well per 250 persons' was achieved well before the deadline of 31 March 2001 and the Self-Employed Mechanics (SEM) scheme was introduced in all 80 blocks of KBK. The Commission, in its proceeding dated 30 August 2006, stressed the importance of proper monitoring of the scheme after its implementation.

ii) **Primary Health Care:** Through the proceedings, mobile healthcare units were opened for the first time—one in each of the 80 blocks of KBK, as noted in the proceeding held on 9 June, 1999. The proceeding dated 14 December, 2000 recorded that after setting up 8 additional Primary Health Care (PHCs) centres and 49 additional mobile health units, the districts had attained full coverage. However, the Commission said that vacancies should remain below 20% in all districts. It also expressed concern about the lack of paramedical staff and the menace of infectious diseases like malaria. The final proceeding on 30 August 2006 noted that the vacancy of doctors had reduced to 19.53%.

iii) **Social Security Schemes:** The Commission, in its proceeding dated 17 February 1998, recommended the removal of the ceiling on persons covered under various pension schemes and expedited distribution of identity cards. The EFP was also supervised through the proceedings. In its proceeding held on 28 January, 1999, the Commission recommended an increase in the daily scale of rice from 200 gm to 250 gm and dal from 25 gm to 40 gm per head under the EFP. Though general improvement in the PDS was noted, further measures to improve coverage were nonetheless advised, after receiving The Special Rapporteur's report.

iv) **Soil Conservation:** The Special Rapporteur had informed in the proceedings held on 10 October, 2002 that 10 out of 20 NWDPRA projects and 70 watershed projects under EAS had been dropped after incurring initial expenditure, and that funds remained underutilized. The Commission saw that the evaluation of the NWDPRA and EAS watershed projects had been handed over to ISRO, Kharagpur, IIM, Kolkata and ISRO, Bangalore (Bengaluru), which would assist in proper execution.

v) **Rural Development Programme:** The implementation of schemes such as the SGSY, SGRY, IAY had not resolved the problem of rural employment and required further monitoring. However, between January, 1998 and March 2000, IAY was well-implemented in all districts; JRY and EAS were executed efficiently in Koraput, Kalahandi, Rayagada and Balangir. The schemes remained just satisfactory in Nabarangpur and Malkangiri, and poor in Nuapada. Sonepur also did not do well under JRY.

vi) **Afforestation:** The Special Rapporteur had noted, as discussed in the proceeding dated 10 October, 2002, the LTAP was being implemented efficiently and that the level of community mobilization was commendable. The final proceeding on 30 August 2006 noted that IIFM, Bhopal was asked to perform an evaluation of the NTMFP policy.

vii) **Land Reforms:** The expert committee on land reforms made recommendations on which the Commission issued directions in its proceeding held on 22 March 2000. Regulation 2/56 was amended to ensure that land could not be transferred from tribals to non-tribals in the state in Scheduled areas (which included all the KBK districts), as noted in the Special Rapporteur's report which was part of the proceedings held on 17 January, 2003. The final proceedings on 30 August 2006 noted that a high-level committee had been formed to bring about similar amendments in the Orissa Land Reforms Act, 1960.[24]

viii) **SC/ST Development:** There was a fall in the dropout rate of SC/ST students in school. Scholarship schemes required more effective implementation.

ix) **Education:** The Special Rapporteur highlighted the poor infrastructure for education as a problem incidental to the proceedings. The Commission recommended that the state should take these observations into account.

The NHRC felt that a systematic process which had been set into motion with utmost clarity and participation of all wings of the government, could not *always* continue under the supervision of the Commission. The system evolved must become a part of government functioning, having self-check mechanisms and transparency. The NHRC, therefore, evolved a monitoring system which the government accepted as being part of its functioning in applying various schemes.

SUGGESTED MONITORING MECHANISM AND ITS ACCEPTANCE BY THE GOVERNMENT

At the end of the hearing before the National Human Rights Commission (on 30 August 2006), it was submitted (by the petitioners' counsel) that after identifying the problems and discovering the solutions, it is only through a continuous monitoring process that significant changes could be achieved. The exercise done before the NHRC set an example for the entire country, as to how perceptible change could be brought about even in a situation where for centuries, people were condemned to suffer and die due to starvation and other related problems.

It was suggested that the process of relief and empowerment which had just started should continue till the people of the KBK region achieve self-sufficiency and human dignity. It was urged before the NHRC that the state should take the opportunity to improve the fate of the people in KBK enabling them to rise from the present situation. It was suggested that this would be possible only by linking planning (and constantly improving upon it) with execution, matching each other's pace, and taking each effort towards visible improvement.

The monitoring process should be created in such a way that it restores confidence in the machinery which is involved in it: that it is in full control of the problems and is determined to end the human suffering. Therefore, complete data and information about planning of the schemes and its execution should be made available to people in a transparent manner, and they should be effectively involved in the process. The idea was to make certain that no person would say that he was without water, no one would die because of non-availability of medicines, and no one would starve because there was no food stock in the emergency feeding centres. It was emphasized that the minimum requirement for survival must be ensured after such a thorough exercise for nearly a decade before the Supreme Court and the NHRC.

In the proceedings on 30 August 2006, the NHRC recorded that the recommendations made by the Commission in its proceedings dated 17 January, 2003 which were broadly based on the suggestions made by Shri Sanjay Parikh, counsel for the petitioners, were accepted by the State of Odisha. The NHRC noted in the proceedings that one of the most vital components of the comprehensive monitoring mechanism, namely, people's participation through public hearings, which was suggested by Shri Parikh, had not been introduced. However, the report of the Special Rapporteur revealed that the recommendation suggested by Parikh, which contained this particular suggestion, was endorsed by Shri MV Rajasekharan, Minister of State for Planning independently. In the Action Taken Report (ATR) filed by the state government, it was stated that the Chief Administrator, KBK and the Deputy Chief Administrator had held public hearings in KBK districts and had heard grievances of the local people. The state government had informed the NHRC that they had decided to disclose key parameters of relevant projects including funds utilization, targets fixed and achieved at prominent places for public scrutiny.

> The Commission commented that (the) monitoring mechanism needs to be institutionalized and strengthened and people's active participation through awareness generation should be encouraged.[26]

The Commission also remarked that a system (as suggested by the petitioners' counsel) of quarterly monitoring methods for the implementation of RLTAP and a monthly special monitoring in the three sensitive areas, namely drinking water, primary health and emergency feeding should be continued on a regular basis.

The Commission observed that the said monitoring mechanism suggested by the Counsel deserved to be introduced with considerable care by the state as it would ensure transparency, public participation and inbuilt check for fixing accountability. The observations in that regard read as follows:

> Shri Sanjay Parikh had expressed his keenness to visit KBK districts at his own expense to see the on-going relief and development work and see how the process of people's empowerment can be expedited. The Commission finds his suggestions in that behalf deserves consideration and directs that a copy of the written submissions and note filed by Shri Sanjay Parikh be forwarded to the State Government, which may find it useful in formulating a comprehensive monitoring mechanism for the RLTAP and since he wishes to visit KBK districts at his own expense, the State Government may assist him to properly conduct the survey by its cooperative attitude.

The monitoring mechanism, suggested as above, endorsed by the NHRC, and accepted by the State of Odisha as an integral part of the institutional monitoring mechanism, has been discussed in the following chapter.

References

1. Coram: Justice Sh. M.N. Venkatachaliah, Chairperson; Sh. Virendra Dayal, Member. [Appendix C] dt. 17.9.1997
2. Coram: Justice Sh. M.N. Venkatachaliah, Chairperson; Sh. Virendra Dayal, Member [Appendix D] dt. 22.10.1997
3. Coram: Justice Sh. M.N. Venkatachaliah, Chairperson; Sh. Virendra Dayal, Member; Justice Sh. V.S. Malimath, Member [Appendix E] dt. 17.2.1998
4. Sen, *Poverty and Famines* (1981), 1.
5. Ibid, 45.

6. Appendix E
7. Coram: Justice Sh. M.N. Venkatachaliah, Chairperson; Sh. Virendra Dayal, Member; Justice Sh. V.S. Malimath, Member.
8. See N.C. Saxena, "Forest Policy and Rural Poor in Orissa", (Delhi: *Wasteland News*, Nov 1995-Jan 1996)
9. Coram: Justice Sh. M.N. Venkatachaliah, Chairperson; Sh. Virendra Dayal, Member.
10. Coram: Justice Sh. M.N. Venkatachaliah, Chairperson; Sh. Virendra Dayal, Member; Justice Sh. V.S. Malimath, Member.
11. Justice Sh. M.N. Venkatachaliah, Chairperson; Justice Sh. V.S. Malimath, Member; Sh. Sudarshan Agarwal, Member.
12. Justice Sh. M.N. Venkatachaliah, Chairperson; Sh. Virendra Dayal, Member.
13. Coram: Justice Sh. M.N. Venkatachaliah, Chairperson; Justice Sh. V.S. Malimath, Member; Sh. Virendra Dayal, Member;
14. Coram: Dr. Justice K. Ramaswamy, Member; Sudarshan Agarwal, Member; Virendra Dayal, Member.
15. Coram: Justice J.S. Verma, Chairperson; Dr. Justice K. Ramaswamy, Member; Virendra Dayal, Member.
16. The Odisha Scheduled Areas Transfer of Immovable Property (by Scheduled Tribes) Amendment Regulation, 2000 came into effect on 4th September, 2002.
17. Odisha Land Reforms Act, 1965, Section 22(5).
18. Coram: Justice J.S. Verma, Chairperson; Justice Mrs. Sujata V Manohar, Member; Virendra Dayal, Member.
19. Coram: Justice J.S. Verma, Chairperson; Justice Sujata V. Manohar, Member; Virendra Dayal, Member.
20. Coram: Dr. Justice A.S. Anand, Chairperson; Virendra Dayal, Member; R.S. Kalha, Member.
21. Coram: Dr. Justice A.S.Anand, Chairperson; Justice Mrs. Sujata V. Manohar, Member; Virendra Dayal, Member; R.S. Kalha, Member.
22. Coram: Dr. Justice A.S.Anand, Chairperson; Dr. Shivaraj V. Patil, Member; Justice Y. Bhaskar Rao, Member; R.S. Kalha, Member.
23. Coram: Dr. Justice A.S.Anand, Chairperson; Dr. Shivaraj V. Patil, Member; Justice Y. Bhaskar Rao, Member; R.S. Kalha, Member; P.C. Sharma, Member [Appendix F]
24. Orissa Scheduled Areas Transfer of Immovable Property (by Scheduled Tribes) Amendment Regulation, 2000; Orissa Land Reforms Act, 1965, Section 22(5).

The Road Ahead : Monitoring Mechanism for the KBK

At this juncture, it is important to consider what the future course of action should be. The efforts reflected in the course of proceedings and their detailed and meaningful hearings proved that change was possible; however, much was left to be achieved in terms of sustaining those efforts and gaining long-term outcomes. Keeping in view the need for a permanent and stable change, the mechanism evolved by the NHRC should be set in the state machinery in such a way that it discharges all responsibilities involving self-check of a binding nature. These include, but are not limited to, regular meetings of the Chief Administrator, District Level Committees and other deemed bodies at the Block/ Panchayat levels. A monitoring system through checklist/tables and digitization of essential data and compliance reports was necessary so that the information could be transferred from the DLC level at least to the Chief Administrator quickly, without any loss of time.

The monitoring mechanism was of two different kinds:

i. **Quarterly monitoring** of (quarterly) targets (of the Annual Plan) relating to RLTAP and all other schemes as well as urgent requirements of a particular district, suggestions of experts, etc.

ii. **Special monitoring** on a monthly basis with regard to health, drinking water and emergency feeding.

i. Quarterly monitoring:

Functions and duties of the Chief Administrator

The Chief Administrator with the help of the Deputy Chief Administrator shall prepare Annual Long Term Plans with quarterly targets for implementation in all the eight districts. This means that the Annual

Plan will be divided into four quarterly action plans. In preparing the Annual Plans, the long term relief plans, schemes of the Central and state government as well as special/urgent requirements/needs of a particular district, will be assimilated. In implementing these Annual Plans—which will be district and area specific —the Chief Administrator will be free to take the help of experts, and to receive/conduct the studies on specific areas with a central focus on empowerment of the people. These eight separate annual plans (with quarterly targets) prepared by the Chief Administrator shall be assigned to the District Level Committee for ensuring implementation and reporting compliance.

- The action plans shall also contain approximate expenses attached to each welfare scheme. Following can be the format (with suitable modifications) in which the District Level Committee shall provide information, at the end of every quarter:

SCHEME	EXPENDITURE	TARGET	SHORT FALL	REASON

- The District Level Committee shall report back to the Chief Administrator about the status of implementation on the quarterly targets. If there is any leftover work, it would be included in the next quarterly action plan with specific directions, if any, by the Chief Administrator.
- The salient points for monitoring of all schemes shall be compiled in the form of a booklet and the same shall be distributed to the concerned officers/officials who are responsible for implementation of various welfare schemes. This booklet shall also fix responsibilities on a particular department/official for such implementation.
- Based on the reported suggestions/recommendations of the Chief Administrator, funds will be released by the state/Central government without any delay so that no calamity of the nature of a starvation death takes place. In order to oversee that the funds are released in time, a separate provision shall be made at the Cabinet Secretariat level.

- **Identification of Vulnerable Areas:** It has been seen that recurrent deaths due to various reasons (malnutrition, lack of food and medical treatment, etc.,) occur in certain areas of KBK districts. A survey on the existing data should be conducted to identify these areas and a regular check should be maintained regarding health, food, water and hygienic conditions in these areas. The District Level Committees, under whose jurisdiction such vulnerable areas fall, should provide a separate note on the monitoring and improvements made in these areas in their report.
- **Awareness and Dissemination of Information:** Dissemination of information, promotion of awareness and public participation are essential and inalienable parts of the development process. These also act as a check on wasteful expenditure and as a control against corruption.
  a) The Chief Administrator shall prepare a booklet (in English, Hindi, Oriya) containing information about various Central and state welfare schemes, brief information about long term developments and the officers who are responsible for implementation of those schemes. This will enable the people to approach the concerned office/officers for obtaining further information on the schemes as well as making suggestions for improvement or making complaints on the shortcomings. This booklet will be distributed to the block level officers, panchayats and people's representatives.
  b) Besides the booklet, information about the welfare schemes at the District, Block and Panchayat level should be disseminated through various means including display of information at Panchayat and other government offices.
  c) The Chief Administrator/District Centre shall also evolve criteria for enlisting credible organizations and individuals who are interested in associating themselves with any particular scheme/ schemes as well as for dissemination of information.
- **Grievance redressal mechanism:** The Chief Administrator shall hold at least one mandatory public meeting every month in any of the districts, giving priority to the area which is vulnerable and is

in any acute problem, so that people can address their grievances and these can be attended to promptly. A brief note of such visits shall also be prepared by the Chief Administrator for any further action and for incorporation in the quarterly target plans. Besides this, the Chief Administrator will also create a Grievance Redressal Committee to attend to the public complaints. These complaints will be attended to within 48 hours. Records of the complaints and follow up action will be maintained. Besides receiving complaints directly, the Chief Administrator will also receive complaints referred to him from the District Level Committees.

Functions and duties of the District Level Committee (DLC)

Each district of KBK shall have one District Level Committee (DLC) to monitor the implementation of the Annual Plan with quarterly targets prepared by the Chief Administrator for that particular district. The DLC shall communicate the requirement of the Quarterly Target Plan for implementation to the concerned government Department/official. The concerned Department/Officers will implement the required scheme at block and village level and shall report the difficulties which a particular Department/Officer comes across during the implementation process including the grievances of the people, to the DLC. The DLC in its compliance report to the Chief Administrator shall not only show the compliance with the Quarterly Target Plan but shall also indicate the special requirement of any particular area which needs immediate attention and solution. Whenever there is an emergency/urgent need and such information is brought to the knowledge of any officer responsible for implementation of the scheme or otherwise at village/block/district level, it will immediately be attended to and if there is any hurdle, the DLC would intimate the same immediately to the Chief Administrator, who in turn, would take action at the highest level including level of the Chief Secretary and Chief Minister.

Saving lives of people in need of food, water or medicine shall be given the highest priority and if, in spite of the information being made available, action is not taken in time, the concerned officer/official shall be held fully responsible for the consequences.

Awareness and dissemination of information

The Office of the District Centre shall also disseminate information with regard to various welfare schemes at Block and Panchayat level. The District Centre shall keep a record of latest information regarding all welfare schemes and officers responsible for implementation of those schemes. This will also be displayed on the board outside the Office of the District Centre. This will not only fix responsibility but also enable people to contact the concerned officer/official in relation to the implementation of a particular scheme.

Public hearing, complaint procedure

The In-charge of the District Level Committee shall hold at least two mandatory public hearings every month giving priority to the areas where there are acute problems or urgent requirements. The DLC shall prepare a report of the public hearing and forward it to the Chief Administrator. Wherever the District Level Committee can solve the problems/grievances, it will do so with promptitude. Local people will be allowed to lodge their complaints with the District Level Committee, which will be attended to immediately, in any case not later than 48 hours. If the District Level Committee receives any complaint with regard to corruption or improper diversification or misappropriation of funds, it will immediately inquire into it and send a report to the Chief Administrator. Prompt action in accordance with law shall be taken in these cases.

Independent monitoring by experts

The state government shall also appoint credible independent or voluntary consultants on proper implementation of the long term schemes like afforestation, soil conservation, water-shed management, nutrition and health so that they can effectively contribute to the success of these schemes. The independent consultants shall also visit the districts/villages to collect further information and give their independent evaluation. The inputs by the independent or voluntary consultants concerning any particular district shall be considered by the Chief Administrator for inclusion in future action plans for the districts.

Special monitoring on monthly basis:

The most important part of this monitoring was to see that people in any part of the KBK region are not left without drinking water because of defunct tube-wells and non-functioning hand-pumps, feeding should not stop because of deficient stock of food grains, or people should not suffer or die because of lack of medicine/medical care.

These issues are: water, health and food. The information will be provided by the District Level Committee in the following format (with suitable modifications):

AREAS OF CONCERN	STATUS	REMARKS
Drinking water: - availability of SEMs - Functional status of tube-wells & hand-pumps - Water quality		
Health: - availability of medicine - treatment facilities - malaria eradication status - polio and other vaccines - incidents of death - other problems Food - availability of quality stock - continuity of feeding disrupted for any reason - other problems		

The monthly reports submitted by the District Level Committees will be considered carefully and with promptitude. Immediate direction shall be issued to the concerned authorities. However, the District Level Committees shall, while monitoring these key areas, give directions for immediate implementation, viz., shortfall of medicines, food stock and non-availability of drinking water In all these areas, the Gram Panchayats shall be integrallyinvolved.

FLOW CHART DEPICTING THE MONITORING MECHANISM FOR ALL SCHEMES THROUGH A QUARTERLY REPORTING SYSTEM

Chief Administrator
and
Deputy Chief Administrator

↓
↓

Preparation of Annual Plan with Quarterly Targets
for each of the Eight districts separately
+
Identification of Vulnerable Areas
+
Dissemination of Information

↓
↓

Annual Plans with Quarterly Targets to be sent to
District Level Committees

↓
↓

Directions to concerned Departments/Officials/Blocks/Panchayats by
the District Level Committee
for implementation/execution of schemes as per
the plans/targets

↓
↓

Implementation at Block/Panchayat level
and reporting to the District Level Committee

↓
↓

Quarterly Action Taken Report prepared by each District Level

Committee to be sent to the Chief Administrator
in a Proforma
+
Requirement of a particular Village/Area/Block

Special monitoring of key areas

District Level Committees preparing Monthly Reports on the Status of

- Water |
- Health | Directions for implementation in
- Food | →→ time bound manner on discovering any
and | shortcoming/deficiency
- Vulnerable Areas |

Emergency situation immediate reporting
↓
Consideration by Chief Administrator
↓
Immediate directions for compliance

Gram Panchayats to be integrally involved in this implementation process.

Check-list for special monitoring in Key Areas

(Health, emergency funding and drinking water)

Along with the monitoring mechanism a check-list for the three key areas, keeping of records and internal reporting procedure was also suggested:

Health

Check-List: Every health center must have all the items mentioned below. It should be the duty of the Incharge of the health center to maintain medicine, equipment and personnel as per the check list and to intimate deficiencies, particularly in consumables like medicine, disposable syringe etc. not later then a week in advance. Besides informing deficiencies in stock/availability, it shall be the responsibility of the Incharge of the health center to place indent for medicines, equipment's etc. to meet with the recurring consumption at least once in a month. The CDMO, upon receipt of reports from the Incharge of the health center, shall arrange for and make available the requisites within 7 days of the date of receipt of the requisition.

Check List to be maintained at the health center

i) Medicines for malaria, diarrhea, scabies, throat infection and T.B. (the diseases to be dealt under 'PanchVyadhiNirakaran Yojana' sufficient for at least 15 days consumption.

ii) Means and methods to preserve the medicines {for eg. Refrigerator etc.}.

iii) Means and methods for application/administration of medicines {for eg. Disposal syringe, saline kit, etc.}

iv) Two sets of basic equipment's like stethoscope, thermometer, BP checking instrument etc.

v) Detailed documents in respect of various medication/vaccination programmes and the time schedule for administration of those programmes.

vi) Minimum staff.

vii) Supply of electricity to equipment's.

viii) Detailed instructions/guidelines concerning special treatment to vulnerable classes {children, old people and pregnant women}.

Note: It shall be the duty of the Incharge of the health center to make a compilation of all such guidelines/instructions for the purposes of records and reference. This compilation should be updated at least once in a month.

ix) List of deficiencies {this list shall be prepared by the Incharge of the health center on weekly basis}.

Every health center, whether PHC, sub PHC or health center under whatsoever name must maintain the aforesaid check list and such check list should be kept as an indicator for verification, if required.

Emergency Feeding

Check List : Every Gram Panchayat should have a check list of :

i. Availability of food stock.
ii. Utensils to cook food.
iii. Personnel to cook and serve food.
iv. Time schedule for preparation and distribution of food.
v. Expected average consumption of ration in a week with corresponding number of persons expected to avail feeding services.
vi. Publicity/awareness of emergency feeding in the locality
vii. Officials responsible to arrange and distribute food.
viii. Wastage of food/ration on previous days.
ix. A detailed list of various programmes concerning public distribution and feeding.

Drinking Water

All recommendations in this respect are formulated on the presumption that the governments have already achieved the target of one source of water for every 150 persons.

Check List : Every Gram Panchayat shall maintain a list of :

i. Sources of water {bore well or hand pump} with corresponding population.
ii. Defunct tube wells and tube wells with installation problems.
iii. Number of SEM's {self employed mechanics}.

The block Headquarters and the DLC should have a detailed and systematic compilation of Gram Panchayat wise check lists.

Supreme Court Order on NHRC Proceedings

The final report of the NHRC along with its recommendations was considered by the Supreme Court in Writ Petition (C) No. 42/1997, Indian Council of Legal Aid and Advice & Ors. v. State of Orissa & Ors.[1] The Supreme Court noted the contents of the NHRC proceedings and observed by its order dated 22.01.2008 as follows:

> The final report with appropriate recommendations has been given by NHRC on 30.08.2006. These recommendations will go a long way in improving the living conditions of the KBK region. The recommendations in the final report of NHRC have been accepted by the state government. The state government has also agreed for an effective monitoring mechanism suggested by NHRC to ensure that the suggestions made by the NHRC are implemented properly and continuously.

Liberty was given to the Petitioners to approach the Supreme Court – its orders having binding effect on the Centre, state and all the other authorities – in case of any difficulty. The recommendations made by the NHRC thus became effective directions, being approved by the Supreme Court.

Reference

1. See Appendix G.

Conclusion

The intensive exercise by the NHRC and the Supreme Court over a prolonged period of more than a decade clearly showed that starvation deaths had occurred because of lack of government initiatives, serious deficiencies in the implementation of welfare schemes and sheer absence of a political will. It was unacceptable, both legally and morally, that a welfare state would dump the problem of starvation deaths on natural calamities like drought, and use outdated methods like a visual estimation of crop-losses to address a complicated problem like death by starvation.

In a nutshell, the NHRC hearings relied on what Amartya Sen referred to as the 'entitlement approach': there should be enough production possibilities, trade opportunities, entitlements vis-à-vis the state and other methods through which people can acquire sufficient food for themselves and their family. It is worth noting again beyond a shadow of doubt that:

> A person starves either because he does not have the ability to command enough food, or because he does not use this ability to avoid starvation. The entitlement approach concentrates on the former problem, ignoring the latter possibility.[1]

This approach was discussed in the Commission's proceedings held on 17 February 1998. These proceedings brought to the surface that the people in the KBK region suffered from poverty and hunger, but essentially, there were no secured means of livelihood to combat hunger, malnutrition and deaths due to starvation. This is inevitable when a state fails to provide legal entitlements to the people. Death due to prolonged hunger is starvation death. But deaths due to common diseases or infirmities which the body cannot withstand because of malnourishment coupled with scarcity of food also count as starvation deaths. The methods adopted by the NHRC addressed the underlying problems that eventually lead to starvation deaths. In these methods, the Commission only ensured a faithful and timely implementation of the government's own schemes, with few changes.

Basic needs like water and food were made available through RWSS and EFPs. The Commission ensured that for a population of 250 persons, at least one source of water (tube well) would be made available. The Commission ensured that Emergency Feeding should continue uninterruptedly and all eligible persons should be included. It was also confirmed the food provided was nutritious, and had the required calorific value. This process was very helpful as an interim measure to prevent starvation deaths.

In order to prevent deaths due to malaria and diarrhoea, the Commission emphasised on the availability of medicines to treat common diseases, even in remote places. For the first time, Primary Health Centres (PHCs) opened in the KBK districts and Mobile Health Units started functioning to reach tribals who could not access PHCs. The Commission directed that doctors and paramedical staff should be available in all the Primary Health Centres. The other actions, namely, SEMs and employment generation under JRY, MWS, IAY schemes were initiated to provide employment and other means of livelihood to the tribals, including the right to the minor forest produce. The provisions of the Orissa Land Reforms Act, 1960 were amended to restore lands to their previous dwellers, the SC/ST communities.

The Commission also defined the right to food from the constitutional perspective, especially, the right to life as enshrined in Article 21 of the Indian Constitution. Over and above, a healthy monitoring mechanism was needed so that the actions initiated by the government continued with the required transparency and accountability.

There was a perceptible change in the situation but that was not enough. It needed to be strengthened further in the years to come.

The sum and substance of the entire exercise was that if there were government will, the problems of poverty and hunger could certainly be addressed, which would also eliminate the possibility of any person dying due to hunger and starvation. If such deaths took place, the government was fully responsible and should be answerable for its constitutional obligations and the public duty doctrine as evolved by the Supreme Court. No longer could the problems of poverty and hunger be shielded by putting the blame on natural calamities. The system which was evolved in these proceedings – to address the problem of starvation and hunger– can also be used for addressing similar problems in order to provide relief and eliminate the factors that breed inequality. The monitoring mechanism suggested in these proceedings was a model which could be replicated with a few alterations in other situations. They are relevant today as well as in the future. Whether it is the problem of migrant workers or the shortage of medicine during Covid pandemic, a structued approch, which is transparent and fixes accountability, with periodical checks, can to a large extent, control the situation. If it is followed in grant of social benefit programes, much of the problems may find a solution.

It would be regrettable, if the situation in KBK, when it ought to improve, deteriorates. If it happens, the responsibility for it would squarely fall on the government machinery and the lack of political will.

These proceedings exposed certain myths created by the government, surprisingly even after Independence when constitutional governance prevails, that people suffer from hunger and starvation due to natural causes. These proceedings also established beyond doubt that if good governance, a clear intention, honesty, firm action and sincerity exist, it would not be difficult to achieve the cherished goal of equitable development.

Reference

1. Sen, *Poverty and Famines*, 45

Appendix A

SUPREME COURT OF INDIA
RECORD OF PROCEEDINGS

Writ Petition (Civil) No. 42/1997

Indian Council of Legal Aid & Advice & ORS	Petitioner(s)
Versus	
State of Orissa & ORS.	Respondent(s)
Date: 28/04/1997	This Petition was called on for hearing today.

CORAM:
Hon'ble The Chief Justice
Hon'ble Mrs. Justice Sujata V. Manohar
Hon'ble Mr. Justice M. Jagannadhar Rao

For Petitioner (s)	Mr. Rajindar Sachar, Sr. Adv. Mr. Sanjay Parikh, Adv.
For Union of India	Mr. TR Andhyarujina, SG Mr. Yatendra Sharma, Adv. Mr. CVS Rao, Adv.
For Respondent (s)	Mr. Indrajeet Ray, Adv Genl., Orissa Mr. RK Mehta, Adv.

Upon hearing the counsel the Court made the following order.

We are informed that O.J.O. Nos. 12207/98 (P.K. Mishra versus State of Orissa and 13637/1996 (Ankul Chandra Pradhan versus State of

Orissa) have been filed by two different individuals relating to the same subject matter as a result of which parallel proceedings are going on in the Orissa High Court. In our opinion, this is inappropriate and not in public interest. The Petitioner in the present case are societies registered under the Societies Registration Act. We consider it more appropriate to examine this question at the instance of the present petitioners in their representative capacity. We, therefore, withdraw to this court those matters from the Orissa High Court to be listed along with W.P (C) No 42/97 on the next date of hearing.

We also informed that the National Human Rights Commission is seized of the matter. The State of Orissa was required to furnish its documents to the Commission which the State Govt., as stated by the learned Advocate General, is to do by 30.4.97. It is, therefore, appropriate that we await the final report of the National Human Rights Commission for further action in this matter. The Learned Advocate General stated that all directions given by the National Human Rights Commission, even when they are of an interim nature, would be promptly complied with by the State Govt.

List the matter on 21.7.97.

Appendix B

SUPREME COURT OF INDIA
RECORD OF PROCEEDINGS

Writ Petition (Civil) No. 42/1997	
Indian Council of Legal Aid & Advice & ORS	Petitioner(s)
Versus	
State of Orissa & ORS.	Respondent(s)
with T.C. No. 9/97 and T.C. No. 10/97	
Date: 21/07/1997	This Petition was called on for hearing today.

CORAM:
Hon'ble The Chief Justice
Hon'ble Mr. B.N. Kirpal

For Petitioner (s)	Mr. Sanjay Parikh Adv,
For Respondent (s)	Mr Altaf Ahmed Addl. Solicitor General with Mr. DS Mehra, Adv, Mr, Jayant Das, Sr Adv with Raj Kumar Mehta

Upon hearing the counsel the Court made the following order.

In view of the fact that the National Human Rights Commission is seized of the matter and is expected to give its report after an enquiry made at the spot, it would be appropriate to await the report.

Learned Counsel for the petitioner submitted that some interim directions are required to be given in the meantime. If that be so, the petitioner is permitted to approach the National Human Rights Commission with its suggestion. As far as this Court is concerned, the matter would be considered even for this purpose on receiving the report of the National Human Rights Commission.

We also consider it appropriate to have the Union of India to appear before the National Human Rights Commission to assist the Commission in a manner as the Commission may require for the purpose of completion of the task of the Commission. The learned Addl. Solicitor General undertakes to ensure prompt steps being taken for this purpose.

List after six weeks, liberty to mention in case of any urgency.

Appendix C

NATIONAL HUMAN RIGHTS COMMISSION
SARDAR PATEL BHAWAN, NEW DELHI

File No. 37/3/97-LD
Date 17th September, 1997

CORAM

Justice Shri M.N. Venkatachaliah, Chairperson Shri Virendra Dayal. Member

PRESENT

1. Shri Sanjay parikh, Advocate with Shri Avinash Mishra for the petitioner;
2. Shri Jayant Das, Sr. Advocate and Shri R.K. Mehta;
3. Shri S. Ghosh, Special Rehabilitation Commissioner, Orissa, Cuttak;
4. Shri Avtar Singh, Advocate for Union of India and Shri Altaf Ahmed. Addl. Solicitor General.

PROCEEDINGS

1. We have heard the counsel for the petitioner as well as for the State and Union Governments, who have taken us through the orders of Supreme Court, dated 28.4.1997 and 21.7.1997.
2. The Commission had in the case pending before it directed a team of its officers to conduct a spot-inspection of the scarcity prone areas of the affected districts of the State of Orissa and make a report. The report of the team was forwarded to the State Government for its comments and the comments of the State Government have since been received. The stage is now set for the Commission's

final recommendations to be formulated and forwarded to the appropriate Government.

3. As, in the meanwhile, the remit of the Supreme Court requires some aspects including some prayears for interlocutory reliefs to be examined in the course of these proceedings, the final order that we may pass in this behalf may itself be treated as the final recommendation of the commission. We requested the learned Counsel for the petitioner as well as those of the State and Union Governments not to perceive the issues in these proceedings as adversarial and contentious but as an occasion for a participatory endeavor to develop a package of programmes, both short and medium term, which will bring out perceptible improvement in the situation within a time frame. The problem of poverty and starvation has been a current human problem in this area. Some of the earlier studies indicate that it is not necessarily one stemming from recurrent natural calamities; but the result of economic deprivation and lack of social opportunity. Indeed some studies seed to point out that rainfall had in fact improved over the years in the area and so had food production. It is, therefore, not realistic to attribute the present human predicament wholly to factors related to drought and scarcity. The key issues appears to be the lack of purchasing power of the affected population. The problem can lend itself to solutions which are comprehensive enough to include an emphasis on the augmentation of the purchasing capacity of the affected populace, by convergence of the social-security programmes and a strict and sincere implementation of employment assurance programmes.
4. It is also to be pointed out that efforts of Government and its agencies however otherwise sincere and devout, might need to be supported by the participation of credible NGO groups in over-seeing and monitoring the relief programme though administrative supervision may continue to be with government. Specific financial allocations shall have to be earmarked and actually made for the relief programmes. There shall also be inbuilt mechanisms for monitoring the programmes through periodical assessments and review of the targeted progress. Reports either to Supreme Court or to the NHRC, as may be indicated by the Supreme

Court, should be a part of the scheme. These periodical reports must themselves have to be subjected to independent expert scrutiny to ensure the credibility of the achievements of the programme.

5. It is necessary that the petitioner as well as respondent Governments (with the assistance of such credible NGO groups as they may choose to involve) hold discussions and develop a package of programmes to be placed before the Commission. We, therefore, request the lerned Counsel to prepare a programme and a plan of action and submit the same to the commission on 25th September, 1997.

The commission at the request of the learned Counsel will sit at 3.00 PM on that day instead of the usual time of 10.30 A.M.

(Justice M.N. Venkatachaliah)
Chairperson

(Virendra Dayal)
Member

Appendix D

NATIONAL HUMAN RIGHTS COMMISSION
SARDAR PATEL BHAWAN
NEW DELHI

Case No. 37/3/97-LD
Date 22nd October, 1997

CORAM

Justice M.N.Venkatachaliah, Chairperson
Shri Virendra Dayal, Member

PRESENT

Shri Sanjay Parikh, Advocate for the petitioners nos. 1 to 3

Ms. Amrita Rangasami, Director, Centre for the Study of Administration of Relief, New Delhi, for petitioner no. 4

Shri Jayant Das, Sr. Advocate and Shri R. K. Mehta, Advocate for the State of Orissa

Shri Avtar Singh Rawat, Advocate for Union of India

Shri P.K. Mishra, Additional Chief Secretary, Government of Orissa

Shri J.K. Mohapatra, Secretary, Revenue, Government of Orissa

Shri Anil Sinha, Joint Secretary, Department of Agriculture & Cooperation

PROCEEDINGS

We have heard Learned Counsel for the Indian Council for Legal Aid and Advice and other petitioners as well as Learned Counsel of the State of Orissa and the Union of India.

Initially, upon taking cognizance of a complaint presented to the Commission by the Minister of Agriculture, Union of India, the Commission deputed a team of its officers for on-the-spot study and to report to the Commission. Shri R. V. Pillai, Secretary-General and Shri Shankar Sen, Director General (Investigation) of the Commission constituted the team and it has submitted its report after a visit and study. The Commission, after perusal of the report, accepted it tentatively subject to the comments of State Government thereon. For that purpose the report was forwarded to the State Government. The State Government has since forwarded its comments. As indicated in the earlier proceedings, the final recommendations to be made by the Commission after taking into consideration the comments of the State Government, would be a part of these proceedings.

It is to be recalled that the Supreme Court of India, by its two orders dated 28.04.1997 and 21.07.1997 made orders directing that the cases before it touching the same subject matter would be considered by it after the National Human Rights Commission had made its recommendations. There were certain prayers for interim relief before the Supreme Court by the petitioners. The implication of the tenor of the order of the Supreme Court of India is that the Commission should also examine these interim prayers and make its recommendations.

Since the recommendations for alleviation of conditions of deprivation in the four districts of the State might call for both short-term and long-term recommendations, the Commission is to consider whether the short-term measures as well as prayers for interim relief should be made immediately and the long-term measures be considered thereafter and suitable further recommendations made.

As far as the long term measures are concerned, it is submitted before us that there is already a "Long Term Action Plan" in existence for the affected districts to be implemented over a period of seven years between 1995-96 and 2001-2002 with an envisaged comprehensive outlay of Rs.1703 crores. As far as this 'Long Term Action Plan' is concerned, the learned Counsel for the Union Government is unable to state whether it has been accepted by both the Centre and State Government and so by whom it is being monitored. Learned Counsel for the Union of

India stated that since the existence of such a long term action plan has been brought to his notice now, he would need a little time to ascertain whether this 'Long Term Action Plan' and the obligations therein have been accepted by the Government of India and necessary financial and administrative sanctions accorded. The Commission is of the opinion that the Counsel should have some time to ascertain the position on this behalf. The Commission finds it necessary to impress upon the Government of India that as the Commission is examining the matters as required by the Supreme Court of India, it is necessary that the Government of India should extend cooperation in resolving the matter expeditiously.

It is submitted before the Commission by the Learned Counsel for the petitioners that till the end of September 1997, an "emergency feeding programme" was in position under which, feeding centres affording nutritional supplements to about 74,545 persons on a one-time-a-day basis for 25 days in a month were functioning. This, according to the State of Orissa, was done with the financial assistance from the Union of India and that the funding has ended with an expiry of September, 1997. Learned counsel for Union of India however says that there was no formal funding of this project by the Union of India but emergency assistance of Rs. 4 crores afforded to the State by the union was utilized by the State for running these feeding centres.

It appears to the Commission that whatever might be the status of that programme in relation to the obligation of the Union of India to fund and support it, it is necessary, as an interim measure, that the feeding centres do continue. The Commission is told by the State Government that though the funding of the scheme formally ended by the end of September 1997, the State Government is continuing with the scheme in anticipation of the extension of the funding support by the Government of India. On the previous occasion, the Commission had asked the Learned Counsel for the Union of India to impress on the Government of India the Commission's view on the necessity to continue the scheme until final recommendations are made. It has now become necessary to formalize that interim recommendation. The Commission is of the view that till the final recommendations are made, the feeding scheme should continue and the pattern of funding shall be as it was before September 1997. The Commission is also told that for the purpose of running the feeding centres the State Government was securing rice at rates applicable to the supplies for persons below poverty line. Since the feeding centres are expected to continue until further orders, the same arrangement shall continue till then.

Call this matter on 4th November, 1997 at 3.00 P.M.

Appendix E

NATIONAL HUMAN RIGHTS COMMISSION
SARDAR PATEL BHAWAN
NEW DELHI

Case No. 37/3/97-LD

Name of the Complainant: Shri Chaturanan Mishra
Union Minister of Agriculture

Reference Case No.2 of 1997- Writ Petition Civil No. 42/97
Indian Council of Legal Aid & Advice and others
Vs.
State of Orissa & Others
(from the Supreme Court of India)

Date: 17th February, 1998

CORAM

Justice M.N Venkatachaliah, Chairperson
Shri Virendra Dayal, Member
Justice V.S.Malimath, Member

PROCEEDINGS

"Starvation is the characteristic of some people not having enough food to eat. It is not the characteristic of there being not enough food to eat."

Amartya Sen in *Poverty & Famines* (1981)

I

1.1 On 23 December, 1996, the Indian Council of Legal Aid and Advice and Others filed Writ Petition (Civil) No.42/97 before the Supreme Court of India, under Article 32 of the Constitution, alleging that deaths by starvation continued to occur in certain districts of Orissa[1] despite the directives given by the Apex Court in its judgement in the case of

Kishen Pattanayak & Another vs. State of Orissa & Others – 1989 Supp (1) SCC 258. The Writ Petition, a copy of which may be seen at Annexure I, sought a number of interim reliefs from the Court.

1.2 When the Writ Petition came before the Supreme Court on 28 April, 1997, the learned Counsel for the petitioner observed that the National Human Rights Commission was seized of the matter of reported deaths by starvation in these districts. He also referred to a report prepared by a team that had been sent by the Commission to Orissa in that connection. He added that the report contained several recommendations and suggestions which, if acted upon, could serve to provide the interim measures needed to prevent the situation deteriorating in the affected districts. In its Order of 28 April, 1997, the Supreme Court consequently stated:

> It is, therefore, appropriate that we await the final report of the National Human Rights Commission. The learned Advocate General stated that all directions given by the National Human Rights Commission, even when they are of an interim nature, would be promptly complied with by the State Government.

1.3 When the matter was listed again before the Supreme Court on 26 July 1997, the Hon'ble Court passed the following Order:

> In view of the fact that the National Human Rights Commission is seized of the matter and is expected to give its report after an enquiry made at the spot, it would be appropriate to await the report.
>
> Learned Counsel for the petitioner submitted that some interim directions are required to be given in the meantime. If that be so, the petitioner is permitted to approach the National Human Rights Commission with its suggestion. So far as this Court is concerned, the matter would be considered even for this purpose on receiving the report of the National Human Rights Commission.
>
> We also consider it appropriate to require the Union of India to appear before the National Human Rights Commission to assist the Commission in such manner as the Commission may require for the purpose of completion of the task of the Commission. The learned Addl. Solicitor General undertakes to ensure prompt steps being taken for this purpose.

1.4 Pursuant to this Order of the Supreme Court, the learned Counsel for the Indian Council of Legal Aid and Advice filed a petition before the Commission on 1 September 1997, making a number of suggestions in regard to interim reliefs (Annexure II). Upon considering this petition, the Commission directed, on 3 September 1997, that notices be issued to all concerned and a letter be addressed to the Union Minister of Agriculture.

1.5 In the latter connection, it is pertinent here to observe that, on 3-4 December, 1996, the National Human Rights Commission had considered a letter from Shri Chaturanan Mishra, Union Minister for Agriculture, concerning a recent visit by him to Orissa. The letter stated that while he was in Balangir, some of the local MLAs and representatives of political parties had complained to the Minister of "starvation deaths during the present drought." The letter from the Minister enclosed a number of press reports alleging deaths from starvation, together with a list of some 26 cases, sent by the District Administration, which asserted that the reported deaths had not occurred as a result of starvation, but had resulted from other causes. The Minister requested the Commission to go into the details of the situation and to undertake an investigation so that an accurate picture could emerge.

1.6 In considering the communication received from the Minister, together with its enclosures, the Commission observed that while the report from the District Administration appended to the Minister's letter took the view that the reported deaths had resulted from illness or natural causes, the press articles suggested the contrary. The Commission accordingly decided that, in the first instance, a team of officers, comprising the Secretary General and the Director General (Investigation) of the Commission should proceed to the affected area to collect the facts of the situation. Notice was also issued to the Chief Secretary, Government of Orissa, to report within four weeks.

1.7 Shortly prior to the departure of the team, the Commission also received a joint memorandum signed by seven Members of the State Legislative Assembly, in which they listed 14 cases of death occurring allegedly as a result of starvation. The memorandum urged the Commission to intervene and to investigate all allegations of such deaths by starvation reported from the affected areas of the State.

1.8 In pursuance of the directions of the Commission, the Secretary General and Director General (Investigation) left Delhi for Orissa on 11 December, 1996 and visited the districts of Nuapada, Kalahandi and

Balangir on 12-14 December,; their supporting staff staying in the area until 17 December, 1996 to gather further data. The team submitted its written report to the Commission on 2 January, 1997, Annexure III. After considering the report carefully, the Commission sought the comments of the State Government on it and also those of the Union Minister, Agriculture. The comments of the State Government were sent to the Commission on 29 April, 1997, under cover of a letter from the Principal Secretary, Revenue and Excise Department; the full text of that response may be seen at Annexure IV. Comments on behalf of the Union Minister for Agriculture were received from the Additional Secretary of that Ministry together with his letter of 22 October, 1997, Annexure V.

II

2.1 The allegations of deaths by starvation and the seemingly recurrent nature of this tragic occurrence in the 'KBK districts', raised issues that were both grave in implication and contentious in substance. After examining the report of its own team and the response of the State Government, and after reflecting on the petitions submitted by the Indian Council of Legal Aid and Advice and Others, the Commission therefore considered it important to conduct in-depth hearings on this entire matter, with the full involvement of all parties concerned. In so deciding, the Commission had in mind the need to lift the consideration of this matter out of the adversarial and contentious *cul-de-sac* in which it might otherwise be trapped, and to transform it into a participative and constructive endeavour designed to develop a package of measures that, within a specified time-frame, would bring perceptible improvement to the lives of the afflicted population in the KBK districts. In pursuit of this objective, the Commission accordingly held 11 hearings, between 3 September 1997 and 29 January, 1998, examining all aspects of the matter, an examination that included, inter alia, economic theories relating to starvation and famine, the economic, social and environmental history of Orissa, and of the 'KBK districts' in particular, over the past decades, the codes and criteria governing the conduct and reaction of State Governments and the Centre to situations such as those obtaining in the 'KBK districts' and, above all, the practical measures that could be taken in the interim, and be dovetailed into Long-Term plans, to end the scourge of deprivation, malnutrition and cyclical starvation in the districts concerned.

2.2 As the present petition before the Commission and the reliefs sought from the Supreme Court essentially request a series of interim measures, this order of the Commission will concentrate primarily on such interim measures, leaving for subsequent consideration as may be needed, the views of the Commission on Long-Term issues.

2.3 This being said, the Commission would like to record, even in its present order, its indebtedness to the path-breaking and authoritative work of Professor Amartya Sen on the question of "Poverty and Famines" which has transformed the understanding of all those who must come to grips, whether on a theoretical or practical plane, with these grave problems. In particular, while considering the allegations of starvation in the 'KBK districts', the Commission had reason to recall Professor Sen's rigorous thesis, now known as the 'entitlement approach', to better appreciate the situation under review. That 'approach' of Professor Sen:

> ..concentrates on the ability of people to command food through the use of the legal means available in society, including the use of production possibilities, trade opportunities, entitlements vis à vis the state, and other methods of acquiring food.[2]

And he had observed:

> Ownership of food is one of the most primitive property rights, and in each society there are rules governing this right. The entitlement approach concentrates on each person's entitlements to commodity bundles including food, and views starvation as resulting from a failure to be entitled to any bundle with enough food.[3]

2.4 In such a view, it is inadequate to explain starvation simply in terms of food availability decline, 'the FAD' approach, or even in terms of the shortage of income and purchasing power. While the latter may be considered a rudimentary way of trying to catch the essence of the 'entitlement approach', it offers only a partial explanation. Understood, according to the 'entitlement approach', a person's ability to command food depends on what he owns, what exchange possibilities are offered to a person, and what is taken away from him or her. The Commission has kept this reasoning in mind in formulating its ideas on this case and, indeed, in setting out the interim measures that, in this Order, it recommends should be implemented in the 'KBK districts'.

III

3.1 The paragraphs that follow indicate the manner in which these interim measures have evolved and been decided upon, the scope of these measures and details concerning them. They also indicate the manner in which the interim measures should be implemented and the monitoring mechanisms that should be set in place in order to ensure the efficiency, integrity and accountability of the effort that must be made.

3.2 The starting point in devising the interim measures was, of course, an analysis of the observations contained in the report of the Commission's team (to which references were made in the petition before the Supreme Court and before the Commission itself), and of the comments received on that report from the State Government and the Union Ministry for Agriculture. While these documents may be seen in full as Annexures III, IV & V, it is necessary here to recall the principal points raised by the Commission's team and the comments thereon.

(i) The Commission's team asserted that, because of the very high level of deprivation existing in the area, along with extensive crop damage, malnourishment, inadequate income levels and insufficient outreach of relief measures, the possibility of deaths having occurred owing to prolonged malnutrition and hunger, compounded by diseases, could not be ruled out. Indeed, out of 21 deaths investigated by the team in the districts of Naupada, Kalahandi & Balangir, 17 were attributable to such causes. The State Government differed on this matter, asserting that the report of the Commission's team did not "bring out clearly any case of death due to starvation." Instead, the State Government stated that instructions had been given to all Collectors to form squads of officials to visit each district each week to enquire into the condition of those who may be ill or weak and to intervene urgently on their behalf.[4] It was added that the Government was supporting a number of supplementary nutrition programmes to ensure that those who were vulnerable for reasons of age or infirmity were fed for 24 days each month. The

Union Ministry referred to the history of drought in western parts of Orissa and the special programmes implemented by the Government of India and the State Government to ameliorate the acute poverty in the area. It was stated that the Government of India had released Rs.54 crores from the National Fund for Calamity Relief (NFCR) to help the State Government, including Rs.4 crore exclusively for the Emergency Feeding Programmes. This was in addition to the normal allocation of Rs 36.76 crore during 1996-97 in the Calamity Relief Fund (CRF) of the State. Since the Government of India was not directly involved with the execution of relief measures, it was added that it would be difficult to comment on the reported deaths by starvation.

(ii) The Commission's team observed that the Old Age/Widow/Disability Schemes run by the State Government were not covering all the deserving cases. The State Government responded that the number of beneficiaries covered by the schemes had been increased from 8,11,980 in November 1996 to 8,73,400 in February 1997 and that the Collectors concerned had been authorized to provide gratuitous relief cards to those who, in their judgement, were in need of emergency succour. The Government of India observed that the State Government had taken the necessary action to enhance the coverage of relevant schemes on the basis of the suggestions of the Commission's team.

(iii) The Commission's team had recommended that the State Government may wish to consider setting up an institutional mechanism at the grass-root level to oversee the relief measures and to add transparency to the administration's programmes. It also felt that there was a need to evaluate the functioning of existing District Level Committees. Pending such action, the team observed that mobile squads should be formed comprising officers of known integrity, to undertake surprise field visits in order to ensure the effective implementation of relief measures. The State Government commented that NGOs were already being associated regularly with the work of Disaster Management Committees and that, following panchayat elections, there was need to fully involve panchayati raj institutions in overseeing relief measures. For its part, the Government of India noted that the observations of the

Commission's team came in the wake of complaints of non-availability of food grains, leakages in the public distribution system and the inadequacy of labour intensive schemes. The Government of India therefore drew attention to the need to make institutional mechanisms work properly, such as the Disaster Management Committees at the State, district and village levels.

(iv) The Commission's team noted the inadequacy of water, both for drinking purposes and more generally; this had resulted in great hardship to the affected population, and even to a shortage of fodder for cattle—the latter circumstance leading to distress sales of livestock. The State Government responded that Rs.3.67 crore had been released from the Calamity Relief Fund/National Calamity Relief Fund for augmenting drinking water in urban areas, 300 tube wells having been sunk against 328 programmes. In addition, under the State Plan and ARWSP, it was stated that, in rural area, the Department concerned was to sink 8200 tube wells, 2000 public tube wells in place of defunct tube wells, and 2447 Anganwadi tube wells. It was added that, against these targets, 5703 tube wells and 346 surface wells had been sunk, and 1140 public tube wells and 616 Anganwadi tube wells had been replaced. It was further stated that the Lutheran World Service (India) was sinking 500 tube wells in the 'KBK districts' and that Rs.2 crore had been released for shallow ponds, surface wells, bunds etc, detailed instructions having been given to Collectors.

(v) A large number of vacant posts for medical staff, particularly in the rural areas of the 'KBK districts', was noted by the Commission's team, which suggested that there was need to redeploy staff and resources to the areas affected by drought. The State Government responded that it had made arrangements to post doctors to the area through ad hoc appointments and changes in staff rules and that it had allocated Rs. 55 lakhs from the CRF to purchase and supply medicines to Primary Health Centres. Further, revenue inspectors, village level workers and gram panchayat functionaries had been asked to visit the affected villages extensively and to report to the Collectors concerned. A sum of Rs. 4 crore had also been allocated from the NFCR for medicines in the drought affected areas. The Government of India took the view that steps had been set in motion to improve the health conditions, in accordance with the observations of the Commission's team.

(vi) The Commission's team observed that large-scale migration was having a negative impact in terms of slowing down the asset-building relief measures, and also adversely affecting the provision of relief measures. The State Government commented that migration by landless, marginal and small farmers was an annual event after the harvesting of the Kharif crop. It was added that such migration resulted from the "pull" of higher wages elsewhere and that the State Directorate of Labour intervened regularly to ensure the improvement of working conditions. The Government of India, while observing that some migration took place even in normal years from among those who sought better employment opportunities and wages, noted additionally that in drought situations there were abnormal rates of unemployment among agricultural workers. It stated that, to deal with such situations, adequate funds were made available under CRF, NFCR and a variety of wage/employment programmes.

(vii) Finally, the Commission's team observed that the 'right level' of sensitivity and awareness was needed to report on conditions of distress in rural areas and to recommend effective relief measures. The team had heard allegations from the local population and elected representatives of the systematic neglect of backward areas and even of partisanship in the sanctioning of relief. Such comments reflected a sense of anger and alienation amongst the people of the area. The State Government responded that relief measures were post-event intervention and, at best, could be ameliorative in nature. Long-term drought proofing measures were required in order to increase the area under assured irrigation. Further, there was need for the harvesting of surplus run-off during the monsoon in order to provide supplementary irrigation, and also for crop substitution (oil seeds, pulses in place of paddy), and watershed treatment that would provide wage employment through the afforestation of the higher reaches, gully control in the middle reaches and a water-harvesting structure in the lower reaches. It was added that the State Government had prepared a Long-Term

Action Plan (LTAP) for the 'KBK districts', covering the period 1995-96 to 2001-02, and that this Action Plan, which had been approved by the Government of India, envisaged a larger flow of funds from the Centre than had hitherto been possible. The State Government indicated that it would welcome the Commission's intervention in securing this larger flow of funds for the Long-Term Action Plan. Government of India, for its part, stated that a large number of poverty alleviation and wage employment programmes were in operation in Orissa, such as the Integrated Rural Development Programme (IRDP), the Development of Women and Children in Rural Areas (DWCRA), the Jawahar Rozgar Yojana (JRY), the Million Wells Scheme and the Employment Assurance Scheme, the National Old Age Pension Scheme, the National Family Benefit Scheme, the National Maternity Benefit Scheme, and the Rural Water Supply and Sanitation Programme. It added that the Long-Term Action Plan (LTAP) was also being implemented for the 'KBK districts.

4. From the above it will be seen that while there was a large measure of agreement on the areas of work in which special efforts had to be made to end the cycle of deprivation and malnutrition in the 'KBK districts— even if not on whether deaths had in fact occurred as a result of starvation—there was a clear need to set down, in a non-contentious and constructive manner, a practical programme of interim measures that would be clearly defined and agreed upon by all of the principal players, a programme that would be readily understood and transparent, and for the implementation of which accountability and regular monitoring would be the *sine qua non*. It would also appear from the above that, despite all of the existing efforts and plans, it remained uncertain as to whether the "bundle of commodities", including food, which Professor Sen considered essential to ensuring that deaths did not occur as a result of starvation, was indeed available to all of the people of the 'KBK districts', especially the most vulnerable.

5. In the 11 hearings that were therefore held by the Commission, following the submission of the petition to it by the Indian Council for Legal Aid and Advice & Others, a practical programme of interim measures was evolved and agreed upon by all of the parties concerned, in a cooperative effort that involved the petitioner, the State Government and the Central Government, working together under the guidance and auspices of the Commission.

6. After due consideration, the Commission also arrived at the view that the interim measures should be undertaken over a period of two years, subject to such periodic reviews as it may consider appropriate and necessary, and that these interim measures should be as follows:

A. Monitoring Arrangements

The key to effective implementation of programmes, however well conceived, is their proper monitoring, which should enhance efficiency, transparency and accountability. The Commission believes that responsibility for such implementation and monitoring must, most appropriately and essentially, be that of the State Government, working through its normal lines of command and control, which must in turn draw fully upon the talents of the officers of the State, panchayati raj institutions and such leaders of civil society, including non governmental organizations, as are in a position to assist with sincerity and integrity. The Commission believes that it is for the State Government to establish the details of such a system of implementation and monitoring for the KBK districts, from the State-level, to that of the district-level and below. This being said, the Commission recommends that, at the State-level, a Monitoring Committee be established under the authority of the Chief Secretary, to guide and supervise the over-all effort. In addition, and without in any way wishing to transgress the normal lines of command and control, the Commission intends to appoint an eminent person to serve as its Special Rapporteur for the KBK districts in order to keep itself fully informed of developments in respect of these districts and to interact, on its behalf, with all concerned authorities, whether at the State, district or other levels, as it may deem to be appropriate and necessary. The name of this Special Rapporteur, in regard to whom the parties have been consulted, will be announced shortly. Costs in respect of the Special Rapporteur will be borne under arrangements to be made by the Commission, it being expected, however, that the State Government will render all possible practical help and cooperation to him in the discharge of his responsibilities.

B. Specificity of Programmes

(1) The Commission has been keen to ensure that the interim measures that are put into effect should be as clearly specified as possible in terms

of location, time-frames and quantitative targets. Thus, while the interim measures will be in effect for a period of two years, subject to review, the Commission has—after careful discussion with all concerned—received from the State Government a specific set of commitments, district-wise and programme-wise, for the period 1.12.1997 to 31.4.1998, in respect of each of the 8 districts belonging to the 'KBK' group. Kindly see, in this connection, the letter of 15 January, 1998 from the Commissioner-cum-Secretary, Government of Orissa, to which are attached detailed tables of the targets for the 'KBK districts', for the five months 1.12.1997 to 31.4.1998, in respect of the programmes relating to Rural Drinking Water Supply, Social Security, Soil Conservation and Primary Health Care (Annexure VI). It has further been agreed in hearings before the Commission that the State Government will provide to the Commission an appraisal in respect of these programmes towards the end of March 1998 and that, by 31 March 1998, it will also submit to the Commission a similar, location specific and time-bound plan for the three succeeding months, namely, May, June, and July 1998. This procedure will be repeated for each succeeding quarter: the appraisal of the preceding quarter and the plan for the succeeding three-months being placed before the Commission a month before the latter commences. In making its assessments of the progress achieved and directions to be given, the Commission will draw upon the advice of its Special Rapporteur.

(ii) Certain comments follow in respect of individual programmes.

C. Emergency Feeding Programme

This was being provided, as a nutritional supplement, to some 74,545 persons, on a once-a-day basis for 25 days a month. After reviewing the suggestions and views on this programme, the Commission is of the opinion that:

(i) The Emergency Feeding Programme, as devised, should continue on a once-a-day basis. However, the programme should be available each day of the month.

(ii) If any needy persons have been inadvertently omitted from the programme, they can be added to those being fed, on the advice of the concerned gram sabha/ gram panchayat, the competent State authorities or the Special Rapporteur of the Commission.

(iii) As the present contents of the feeding programme should, according to all reports, be improved upon both in terms of the types of food offered and the calorific value of the food, the Commission recommends that the Monitoring Committee examine this matter carefully, drawing upon the best available advice of competent nutritionists and other experts in such matters, and make the necessary improvements.

(iv) The food is at present prepared by Anganwadi workers and this should continue. To the extent that additional personnel are needed to help, they should be drawn from the local population, so that employment is generated under the appropriate schemes e.g., the Jawahar Rozgar Yojana (JRY).

(v) The State Government has requested the Commission to give directions to the Central Government to release the funds due from the latter for the continuation of the Emergency Feeding Programme upto 30 April, 1998. When considering a similar request on 22 October, 1997, the Commission asked the learned Counsel of the Union of India to impress upon the Government of India the Commission's view on the necessity of continuing the scheme until final recommendations were made. The Commission would now like to reiterate, as it did in its order of 22 October, 1997, that the feeding scheme should continue and that the pattern of funding shall be as it was before September 1997. Further, as also stated on 22 October, 1997, since the feeding centres are expected to continue until further orders, the Commission trusts that, for the purpose of running such centres, the State Government will also continue to be able to secure rice at the rate applicable to supplies for persons living below the poverty line.

D. Old Age Pensions, Disability Pensions & Other Social Security measures

(i) The Commission is of the view that all those who qualify for old age pensions, disability pensions and other social security measures under the existing criteria governing such schemes, should be included among the beneficiaries. It was agreed in the hearings that these criteria would not be sought to be modified for purposes of the present exercise. The State Government has, however, through its letter of 5 February 1998 addressed to the Commission by its learned Counsel, indicated that the number of those who would qualify for assistance under the existing criteria of the National Old Age Pension scheme, would be 47,959 persons more than the 56,579 beneficiaries so covered at present under that scheme for the 'KBK districts.' The Commission recommends that the proposal of the State Government in regard to this additional number of beneficiaries, which has already been submitted by it to the Central Government, should be acted upon expeditiously, in light of the Commission's observation made above.

(ii) As there have reportedly been delays in the monthly disbursement of pensions and such benefits, the Commission trusts that the monitoring system established by the State Government will ensure that such delays do not recur. The system of distributing identity cards to beneficiaries should also be expedited, as one means of off-setting such delays.

E. Employment Generation in Agriculture, Ecological Security, Soil Conservation, Irrigation and other schemes

(i) Without, at this stage, going into questions relating to the implementation of the Long-Term Action Plan for the 'KBK districts,' the Commission has noted the specific undertakings contained in Annexure VI, not least insofar as they relate to employment generating activities. Here again, learning from past experience, the Commission urges the tightening of monitoring systems along the lines set-out earlier in this Proceeding.

(ii) Further, in the light of the programmes being implemented, it appears to the Commission that the benefits of many of these could be maximized by linking them more consciously to employment generating projects. By way of illustration, the water-supply scheme (including the repair and maintenance of handpumps), the distribution of medicines in the Public Health Schemes, soil conservation and irrigation works, all lend themselves to such a purpose, as would afforestation programmes, which could be included in the effort, together with the revival of water-conservation installations of an earlier period which have fallen into disrepair.

(iii) Here again, the Commission has been informed of delays in regard to payments to those engaged in employment generating programmes. The Commission trusts that this too will be set right by the Monitoring Committee of the State Government, for it negates the whole purpose of the endeavour if delays in payment are allowed to compound the suffering of those who are dependent on such programmes.

F. Drinking Water

The quantitative plans of the State Government are fully spelt out in their various submissions to the Commission. Further, the precise plans for the five-months ending 30 April, 1998 are contained in Annexure VI. The Commission sees no need therefore to comment on these plans any further at this stage, except to note that, in the hearings before it, mention has repeatedly been made to the need to maintain and keep in good-repair the tube wells and hand pumps that already exist but that are often in unusable condition. The Commission trusts that the Monitoring Committee will give this matter its attention as well, and will endeavour, not least through the training of local personnel and an improvement in logistical facilities, to remedy the situation.

G. Public Health

(i) Here too, the quantitative plans have been submitted to the Commission and require no specific comment at this stage. The Commission has taken note of these, and of the new regulations that the State Government is enforcing to ensure the posting of medical staff to rural areas. The Commission would like to observe, however, that it is deeply concerned at the deleterious, indeed devastating effects of malnutrition on young women and mothers, that is taking a cruel toll on them and that is leading, in addition, to an unacceptably high incidence of low-birth weight amongst the children being born, a deficiency that in turn prevents the full development of their human potential. The Commission strongly recommends that the potential Monitoring Committee take maximum steps to ensure that measures are taken in the 'KBK districts' to provide the iron and iodine supplements and the vitamin A that is required by young women to prevent such needless harm from occurring.

(ii) Further, given the perilous nutritional conditions prevailing in the 'KBK districts, the Commission recommends that a health-cum-nutritional survey be undertaken for these districts by an independent agency, such as the Nutrition Foundation of India.

H. Land Reforms

(i) The matter of land reforms falls within the context of long term measures needed for the 'KBK districts' and, at this stage, the Commission is not entering into the details of those measures or of the implementation of the Long-Term Action Plan.

(ii) It has, however, been pointed out to the Commission in the hearings that the issue of land reforms is inextricably linked to the future well-being, or decline, of these districts. It has accordingly been urged that the State Government should, even at this stage, be requested to constitute a Committee to examine all aspects of the land reform question in the 'KBK districts'. The Commission sees value in this suggestion and urges the State Government to constitute such a Committee with the request that it give its report, within a fixed time-frame, on the measures that should be taken in these districts to remedy the present situation that is marked by a lack of land reforms, the alienation of land, migration and numerous other concomitant ills.

I. Other Observations

(i) The State Government has expressed its concern that, with the elections to the Lok Sabha having been announced and now underway, the implementation of these interim measures should not be affected by the restrictions imposed by the Model Code of Conduct This Commission would like to make clear that the measures envisaged have been evolved, and their implementation commenced, well prior to the announcement of the elections. Accordingly, it expects that the implementation of these measures will proceed unhindered by any such restrictions.

(ii) It remains of course open to the petitioner, and to the other parties, to approach the Commission on any additional matters which they may wish to bring to the attention of the Commission for further directives.

7. Finally, the Commission wishes to place on record its deep appreciation of the most able and constructive cooperation that it has received throughout its consideration of this matter from the learned Counsels appearing before it: Shri Sanjay Parikh for the petitioner, Shri Jayant Das and Shri Raj Kumar Mehta for the State Government of Orissa, and Shri Ajay Kumar Vali and Shri Avtar Singh Rawat for the Union of India. The Commission is also indebted to Dr. Amrita Rangasami, Director, Centre for the Study of Administration of Relief for her most thoughtful presentations and submissions. At every stage of the proceedings, the Commission has also received the fullest cooperation of the senior officers of the State and Central Governments, whose presence it has requested. Their collaborative effort has enabled the Commission to set-out the interim measures recounted above through a process that has been notably non-adversarial and cooperative in its approach and outcome. As indicated earlier, the Commission will revert to the longer-term issues raised in respect of the KBK districts separately and at a later stage.

8. A copy of these Proceedings may be forwarded to the Registrar of the Supreme Court of India for being placed in the records of the file of the Writ Petition (Civil) No.42/97 pursuant to Orders therein dated 28 April, 1997 and 26 July 1997. The Commission directs that these recommendations be implemented by the State of Orissa and the Union of India forthwith. The Commission would further clarify that the recommendations made by it pursuant to the Orders of the Hon'ble Supreme Court of India would be subject to such other or further directions as the Hon'ble Supreme Court may be pleased to issue in the matter.

References

1. The reference being to what are popularly known as the KBK Districts which now, in fact, comprise the eight districts of Kalahandi. Nuapada, Balangir, Sonepur, Koraput. Malkangiri, Nabarangpur and Rayagada.
2. Prof Sen, opus cited.
3. Prof Sen, opus cited
4. It is relevant to note, however, that the State Government's report gives its views on only 6 of the 21 cases investigated by the Commission's team.

Appendix F

NATIONAL HUMAN RIGHTS COMMISSION
NEW DELHI

Name of the Complainant:	Shri Chaturanan Mishra
Case No.	37/3/97-LD
Coram:	Dr. Justice A.S Anand, Chairperson
	Dr. Justice Shivraj V Patil, Member
	Justice Shri Y. Bhaskar Rao, Member
	Shri R.S. Kalha, Member
	Shri P.C Sharma, Member

PROCEEDINGS

These proceedings are in the nature of final assessment and stock-taking of the implementation of various recommendations/ suggestions made by the Commission to alleviate the sufferings in the districts of Koraput, Balangir and Kalahandi (hereinafter called KBK districts) of State of Orissa ravaged by drought, hunger, poverty and disease and have, therefore, to be read in continuation of various earlier proceedings of the Commission in this case. The final assessment/stock-taking is based on the final hearing in the matter which took place on 18h of July, 2006 and in particular, on the report of the Special Rapporteur of the Commission, Shri Chaman Lal, and the written submissions subsequently filed by Shri Sanjay Parikh, learned counsel for the petitioners dealing with ground realities of programmes undertaken to carry out the directions/ recommendations/suggestions made by the Commission from time to time. It may be recalled that the Commission has been monitoring the situation in the KBK districts on a continuing basis and examining the quarterly Performance Appraisal Reports relating to the achievement of physical and financial targets. It is, however, desirable that a brief reference to the background of the case is noticed in these proceedings for sake of continuity and clarity.

This case has its origin in the reports of starvation deaths in districts of KBK brought to the notice of the Commission by Shri Chaturanan Mishra, the then Union Minister for Agriculture in December, 1995 and the following observations of the Supreme Court of India dated 26 July, 1997 in a Writ Petition filed by Indian Council of Legal Aid and Advice and others, W.P. (Civil) No. 42/97:

> In view of the fact that the National Human Rights Commission is seized of the matter and is expected to give its report after an inquiry made at the spot, it would be appropriate to await that report.
> Learned Counsel for the petitioner submitted that some interim directions are required to be given in the meantime if that be so, the petitioner is permitted to approach the National Human Rights Commission with its suggestion. So far as this Court is concerned, the matter would be considered even for this purpose on receiving the report of the National Human Rights Commission.
> We also consider it appropriate to require the Union of India to appear before the National Human Rights Commission in such manner as the Commission may require for the purpose of completion of the task by the Commission. The learned Addl. Solicitor General undertakes to ensure prompt steps being taken for this purpose.

Pursuant to the directions of the Supreme Court, the Indian Council of Legal Aid and Advice filed a petition before the Commission on September 1, 1997. The petitioner made a number of suggestions in regard to grant of interim relief to the affected persons so as to mitigate their sufferings arising on account of lack of freedom from hunger and denial of the right to food, drought and disease.

The expression 'right to life' contained in Article 21 of the Constitution of India has been judicially interpreted as not merely a life of survival or animal existence but a life with human dignity. It follows, therefore, that the State is obliged to provide at least those minimum requirements which are essential to enable a person to live with human dignity and the right to food is, in the opinion of the Commission, inherent to live with dignity. International Covenant on Economic, Social and Cultural Rights of 1966, to which India is a party, expressly recognizes, in Article 11, the right of everyone to an adequate standard of living, including adequate food

In its proceedings dated 17 February, 1998, the Commission set out a practical programme of interim measures agreed upon by all the parties concerned that involved the petitioners, State Government and the Central Government working together in a cooperative effort. The programme involved at that hearing covered the following matters:

1. Rural Water Supply Schemes;
2. Public Health Care;
3. Social Security Schemes which included Old-age/Widow Disability Pension Scheme, Emergency Feeding Programme, Supplementary Nutrition Programme, Public Distribution System and National Family Benefit Scheme;
4. Water and Soil Conservation Measures; and
5. Rural Development Schemes such as Jawahar Rozgar Yojana Employment Assurance Scheme, Indira Avas Yojana, etc.

These were to be addressed by the State and Central Government as interim measures. The State Government was required to submit Performance Appraisal Reports to the Commission which were being examined and the case was dealt with as a Court case.

The Commission had, at the initial stages of the case, made it quite clear to all the parties that the issue under consideration was not of an adversarial nature and should be treated as an exercise of a participative and constructive endeavour designed to develop a package of measures that could bring about perceptible improvement in the lives of the affected population in the KBK district of State of Orissa. It deputed a team of officers comprising the Secretary General and the Director General (Investigation) to visit the affected areas for an on-the-spot inquiry into the reports of deaths by starvation. The team found that out of 21 deaths investigated, 17 were attributed to high level of deprivation existing in the area as a result of extensive crop damage, inadequate income levels and insufficient out-reach of relief measures. It also found that prolonged malnutrition and hunger compounded by disease had played the contributory factors. The Commission, after considering the report of the team, called for comments from the State Government as also from the Union Minister for Agriculture on that report. This was followed by in-depth hearings of the entire matter with the participation of all concerned parties.

The Commission had in its earlier proceedings of 17th February, 1998 (supra) requested the State Government to constitute a Committee to examine aspects of the Land Reform question in the KBK districts asserting that "the key to effective implementation of programmes, however, well-conceived, was their proper monitoring and that this would enhance efficiency, transparency and accountability." The Commission requested the State Government to constitute a State Level Monitoring Committee headed by the Chief Secretary to guide and supervise the efforts on that behalf. Shri Chaman Lal, Special Rapporteur of the Commission, was directed to assist the Commission so as to keep itself fully informed of various developments in respect of the KBK districts and also to interact, on its behalf, with the concerned authorities at the State, district and other levels.

The details of various hearings and the background of the case have been elaborately dealt with by the Commission in its proceedings of 17 January, 2003 and are not being repeated in these proceedings. The Commission by that order had underscored the basic commitment of the State as well as the civil society to eradicate poverty and hunger which constitutes an affront to the dignity and worth of human beings. The proceedings of 17 January, 2003 also reflect the status of short term measures of two year period ending 31 March, 2001 and the ongoing progress of the long term action plan re-named as Revised Long Term Action Plan (RLTAP) covering the period from 1998-99 onwards. 11 key sectors were expected to be covered by the RLTAP. This was done in consonance with the view taken by the Commission in its proceedings dated 17th February, 1998, wherein the Commission had indicated its intention to dovetail the short-term measures into long-term plans "to end the scourge of deprivation, malnutrition and cyclical starvation" in the KBK districts.

The Commission, with the able and untiring assistance of its Special Rapporteur, Shri Chaman Lal, has been monitoring the situation in the three districts on a continuing basis, seeking and examining the quarterly Performance Appraisal Reports (PAR) relating to the achievement of physical and financial targets. Shri Chaman Lal, Special Rapporteur, as per directions of the Commission, visited KBK districts on various occasions to see for himself the ground reality and verify accuracy of the PAR submitted by the State Government to the Commission. Shri Chaman Lal, accordingly, after carrying out the field study has been submitting his reports from time to time. The reports submitted by the Special Rapporteur were forwarded by the Commission to the State Government for their response after considering which the Commission gave specific directions as were found necessary. The suggestions made by Shri Sanjay Parikh, counsel for the petitioners, regarding Long-Term Plan/Scheme to alleviate poverty in Orissa as well as submissions made by Dr. Amrita Rangasami, were also forwarded to the State Government and a comprehensive reply was sought from it. Shri Jayant Das, Senior Advocate for the Government of Orissa, was requested to organize a meeting jointly with the Chief Secretary and other concerned officials from the Government of Orissa with Shri Chaman Lal, Shri Sanjay Parikh and Dr. Rangasami to arrive at a consensus on as many issues as possible.

The State Government submitted a detailed report regarding the short term and long term measures taken in accordance with the recommendations/suggestions of the Commission. However, before concluding the case before it on the basis of the action taken reports submitted by the State Government, the Commission considered it appropriate to get the ground realities assessed to record what had been achieved and what further recommendations or suggestions, if any, need to be made by the Commission.

Therefore, vide its proceedings dated 28 July, 2005, the Commission directed the Special Rapporteur, Shri Chaman Lal, to once again visit the districts in the KBK region for verifying on the ground the implementation of the Long-Term and Short-Term Plans as stated by the State in its report and submit his report so that the matter could be finally concluded and report submitted to the Hon'ble Supreme Court. The Special Rapporteur, accordingly, visited the KBK districts from 11 to 23 December, 2005 and submitted his report dated 13.3 2006. The report of Shri Chaman Lal was forwarded to the Government of Orissa and others on 27.3.2008 for response and appropriate follow-up action. The comments/compliance reports from the State Government were received vide a FM06-25528RAOM dated 10.7.06.

During the final hearing of the case on 18 July, 2006, Shri Sanjay Parikh, Advocate for the petitioners, Shri R.K. Mehta, Advocate for the State of Orissa, Shri Ajay Kumar Vali, Advocate, Ministry of Agriculture, Government of India, Dr. Ms. Amrita Rangasami, Director, CSAR, Shri G.B Mukherji, Chief Administrator, KBK Region, Shri TK Mishra, Principal Secretary, Revenue Deptt., Government of Orissa and Dr. RV Singh, Special Secretary, Planning & Coordination Department, Government of Orissa were heard. Shri Sanjay Parikh submitted that he may be permitted to file written submissions after studying the reports of the Special Rapporteur and the State Government and taking into account the presentations made during the final hearing. He was permitted to do so.

At the hearing, after recounting the background of the case, the Special Rapporteur made a presentation of his report based on his visit to all the 8 districts of KBK, Orissa from 11-24 December, 2005, to verify on ground the up-to-date status of Revised Long-Term and Short-Term measures as submitted by the State Government to the Commission during the hearing of the case on 28 July 2005. During his presentation, the Special Rapporteur elaborately dealt with the comments/compliance reports received from the State Government in the light of the verification made by him during his field visit.

Shri GB Mukherji, Chief Administrator, KBK Region, during the hearing responded to the issues raised by the Special Rapporteur in his presentation and Shri Tarun Kant Mishra, Principal Secretary, Revenue Department and Dr. RV Singh Special Secretary, Planning and Coordinating Deptt., also made their submissions before the Commission to highlight the measures taken by the State.

In the light of the submission and presentations made at the hearing of 18 July, 2006, the Commission, while noticing thc measures taken by the State Government, proceeded to point-out shortcomings, if any, and make further recommendations with regard to the factors noticed by it in its earlier proceedings, particularly those of 17 February, 1998, 10 October, 2002 and 17 January, 2003.

RURAL WATER SUPPLY AND SANITATION (RWSS)

The Commission has noted with satisfaction the progress of implementation of the suggested revised norms of providing tube wells in the KBK districts. It is seen that the target of providing one tube well for a population of 250 persons in all the KBK districts had been fully achieved well before the time limit of 31 March 2001, set for the completion of the short-term measures. The Commission is also pleased to be informed about the introduction and efficient execution of the Self-Employed Mechanic (SEM) Scheme in all the 80 Blocks of the KBK. It is a matter of satisfaction that the administrative and financial control over the SEMS would soon be transferred to the Panchayati Raj Institutions. The Commission, however, expects the State Government to give its serious attention to the following issues

- Vacancies of SEMS mentioned in the report of the Special Rapporteur should be filled immediately by selecting suitable candidates and imparting them required training.
- The Rural Development Department must ensure early development of a protocol to define the types of repairs to be undertaken by the SEMS and RWSS maintenance outfits and procurement and supply of spare parts. The need for strengthening of Quality Monitoring and Surveillance Programme highlighted in the report of the Special Rapporteur needs to be addressed urgently and we recommend accordingly.

PRIMARY HEALTH CARE

The Commission is concerned about the generally poor state of health care facilities still prevailing in the KBK region as pointed out by the

Special Rapporteur with sufficient details. Dr. Amrita Rangaswami, Director, CSAR has also made a specific mention of these deficiencies in her submissions.

The State Government had, during the earlier hearings, stated before the Commission that vacancies of Medical Officers and paramedical staff would not be allowed to exceed 20% in the KBK region. The presentation of Special Rapporteur, however, shows that vacancies of Medical Officers in the region are well above this ceiling in at least six out of the total 8 districts. The Commission was told by the Chief Administrator KBK in the course of his submissions, during the final hearing, that with the posting orders of 54 more doctors to KBK districts after the visit of the Special Rapporteur, the overall vacancy positions of Medical Officers in KBK districts have already dropped to 19.35%. While that is a positive, the ceiling of 20% is still being exceeded in Kalahandi (22.60), Malkangiri (29.21), Navarangpur (31.63) and Nuapada (28.57). Moreover, the improvement in health care facilities by issuing posting orders of medical officers, as claimed, cannot be accepted only on the basis of issuing of posting orders until the exact position about the number of doctors who actually join duty becomes known. Past experience tells us that it is not certain that all the doctors posted to the KBK region would actually join there. **The Commission, therefore, recommends to the State Government to give its utmost attention to appointment of medical officers in the KBK region. The shortage of medical Specialists in these districts is also required to be attended to at least by posting Additional Specialists from outside and carrying out internal adjustment to ensure even distribution.** The opening of additional Sub Centres in all the districts as per 2001 census figures is another important health care matter for the State Government to consider. **The implementation of the Immunization Programme requires to be strengthened by effective supervision and evaluation of performance against the prescribed targets and we expect the State Government to act positively and take time-bound action.**

The Commission is distressed to note the failure of the State Government in effectively combating the menace of Malaria and even

Diarrhoea in this region which keeps on recurring. The Commission hopes that the State Government would take immediate remedial measures to address the concerns pointed out by the Special Rapporteur not only about under-reporting of Malaria deaths and complaints about free supply of medicines at the Government Health Institutions but also taking effective steps to eradicate Malaria and Diarrhea. While agreeing with the Chief Administrator KBK about the need for innovative awareness generation programmes with an emphasis on preventive health, the three components of health care—preventive, curative and promotive—must receive full attention of the Government in chalking out health care strategies.

SOCIAL SECURITY SCHEMES

The Commission has noted with certain satisfaction the expansion and efficient execution of various Pension Schemes as well as the Supplementary Nutrition Programme (SNP). The ICDS Programme requires greater attention in view of its crucial significance to the status of health of mother and child. **There is an urgent need for reviewing the locations of Anganwadi Centres and their proper management, especially in remote areas, to ensure that the benefits of the scheme reach all the targeted beneficiaries.**

The Commission had, vide its proceedings of 28th January, 1999, recommended an increase in the supply of daily scale of rice from 200 to 250 gm. and Dal from 25 to 40 gm per head under the Emergency Feeding Programme (EFP). While the Commission's recommendation was accepted in respect of supply of quantity of Dal, the State Government stated that as per the opinion of the Nutrition Experts, the quantity of rice was sufficient. The report of the Special Rapporteur has, however, brought with touching clarity an urgent need for increasing the supply of quantity of rice, as recommended by the Commission, earlier. The comments/compliance report dated 10.7.06 does not contain any encouraging response to this issue. The Commission, however, takes on record the submissions of the Chief Administrator made during the hearing, that a decision has now been taken to implement the recommendation of the Commission in this behalf and increase the quantity of rice.

The report of the Special Rapporteur also points out that the BPL Card holders in Orissa are receiving only 25 kg rice per family per month as against their entitlement of 35 kg because of a huge difference in the estimation of BPL families identified by the Government of India and the State Government. It was clarified during the hearing by the Principal Secretary Revenue that the Government of India was allocating BPL rice to the States on the basis of 1993-94 poverty estimates of the Planning Commission as on 1st March 2000 as projected by the Registrar General of India. Accordingly, allocations of Orissa have been limited to 32.98 lakh estimated BPL households whereas the State Government has in its door to door survey identified 50.19 lakh BPL households. Due to this reason, the State Government is compelled to allocate only 25 kg of rice per month to a BPL family, though the poorer category of BPL families covered by Antyodaya Anna Yojana (AAY) are being provided 35 kg of rice a month.

The Commission requests the Government of India, through its Counsel, to appreciate the request made by the State Government and suitably enhance the allocation of BPL rice @ 35 kg per month to 50.19 lakh BPL households, until the findings of 2002 survey at present under the scrutiny of the Supreme Court are finalized.

The Special Rapporteur has also pointed out that there was a huge pendency of unsettled claims under the National Family Benefit Scheme (NFBS) in every district. Comments/Compliance Report dated 10.7.06 shows that the Govt of India had been approached by the State Government to release a sum of Rs. 50 crore to clear up the pending claims of 53,254 beneficiaries under NFBS in Orissa which includes 12,268 belonging to KBK districts. **We wish to point out that the Government of India has an obligation to pay that amount. The Commission requests the Government of India (Women and Child Development Department) to take urgent action on that behalf.**

KBK region has been equated with the country's most backward districts. It is, therefore, appropriate that not only funds are released by the Government of India in time but also that the same are increased, if necessary, but surely not curtailed.

The Commission appreciates the efforts of the State Government to efficiently operationalise Annapurna and Antyodaya Schemes under the Public Distribution System. Proposed involvement of Village Mother's Committees in the monitoring of SNP and EFP is indeed a commendable initiative of the State Government. These Committees can ensure effective monitoring of Take Home food stuff for children in the 0-3 years age group. The Commission records its satisfaction about steps taken for involvement of the Gram Panchayats (GPs) and village Women Self Help Groups in running the PDS.

SOIL CONSERVATION DEPARTMENT

The observations of the Special Rapporteur regarding the execution of NWDPRA and EAS Watershed Projects have been invariably critical of the performance of departmental works. The proper execution of such works calls for serious remedial action. The Commission is pleased to note that the suggestion regarding the evaluation of these projects has been accepted by the State Govt and expert bodies like ISRO, Kharagpur, IIM, Calcutta and ISRO, Bangalore have been engaged for evaluation. Such an evaluation will help not only in fixing accountability for the past deficiencies and irregularities but also would act as a check on the on-going NWDPRA, IWDP and other watershed projects in KBK districts under the RLTAP.

RURAL DEVELOPMENT PROGRAMME

While noting with satisfaction the efficient execution of various Rural Development schemes, such as SGSY, SGRY, IAY, the Commission finds that these have not really helped much in dealing with the problem of rural unemployment. It is hoped that an efficient implementation of the recently introduced National Rural Employment Guarantee Scheme extended to the KBK districts would bring about the desired change.

The Commission, therefore, recommends that allotment of targets to the districts and performance appraisal should be made on quarterly basis, as was evolved by the Commission for the short-term measures. Besides facilitating effective monitoring, this would ensure smooth and progressive utilization of funds and avoid rush of expenditure towards the end of a financial year.

AFFORESTATION

The Commission has noted with appreciation the generally satisfactory execution of the LTAP with people's participation. The observations of the Special Rapporteur about the reluctance of the subordinate staff to make the members of VSS aware of their ownership rights over the minor forest produce calls for launch of a sensitisation programme for the field functionaries and intensification awareness generation programmes for the villagers involved in these projects. The Commission finds that the State Government has decided to give an impact evaluation study to IIFM, Bhopal in response to the suggestion regarding the need for evaluation of the new NTMFP policy introduced by the State Government vide its notification dated 31.3.2000. This is a step in the right direction.

LAND REFORMS

In its proceedings of 17 January, 2003, the Commission had expressed its satisfaction about the amendment of Regulation 2 of 1956 which completely banned the transfer of land from tribals to non-tribals in scheduled areas of the State comprising 13 districts including 8 districts of KBK. However, the report of the Special Rapporteur, after his latest field visit, shows that the follow-up action on the implementation of amended provisions to find cut cases of land alienation, particularly fraudulent cases of sale/transfer of land from tribals to non-tribals is not very encouraging. The Commission notes with a certain amount of regret that not much has been done so far for changing land relationships to the legitimate advantage of the tribal population whose livelihood system is dependent on land resources. The matter deserves to be taken up with utmost urgency. As suggested by the Special Rapporteur, a certain proportion of decided cases of land alienation, say 5 to 10 per cent, should be physically verified on the ground to see whether land ordered and restored to the tribal owners is actually being held by them or not. This would ensure that the system is properly monitored and does not merely remain a "paper transaction."

With a view to derive the intended benefit of these progressive measures for the benefit of the tribal population, the Commission recommends that special drives should be launched in all districts and performance of District Collectors evaluated accordingly. The laudable objective of the amendment should not get lost due to any slackness in its implementation.

The Commission reiterates its recommendations made in its earlier proceedings of 17 January, 2003 regarding implementation of the comprehensive suggestions made by the Expert Committee on Land Reforms. The Principal Secretary, Revenue, during the final hearing, informed the Commission about a series of measures initiated by the State Govt. to introduce land reforms and referred to 'Mission Bhumi', 'Project Vasundhara' and the Land Pass Book Schemes in that connection properly for deriving best results. The measures introduced need to be monitored.

The Commission wishes to remind the State Govt about its commitment to bring forth amendments in tune with amendment 2/56 in the Orissa Land Reform Act. 1960. The Principal Revenue Secretary informed us during the hearing that a High Level Committee headed by the Chief Minister has been set-up to examine the relevant provisions of Regulation 2/56 in order to bring forth further amendments in order to safeguard the interest of the tribals and that after the Committee's Report is received and examined, the Government would process the matter relating to bringing forth amendments in the Orissa Land Reform Act, 1960, so as to ban completely the transfer of tribal land to non-tribals in non-schedule areas. The Commission recommends that appropriate steps be taken in this behalf expeditiously.

ST/SC DEVELOPMENT

The Commission appreciates the efforts taken towards improvement of educational facilities for SC/ST students. Better results, as compared to the previous years, in class Xexamination is a proof of sincere efforts having been taken in the area. A significant fall in the drop out rate of SC/ST children is also a matter of satisfaction and shows the seriousness with which the issue is being tackled. However, it appears that the benefits of scholarship schemes have not reached all the SC/ST students.

The Commission, therefore, recommends that all the students in schools run by the ST/SC Department should receive the benefit of the scholarship scheme. It requests the Govt. of India to allot BPL rice in sufficient quantity to meet full requirements of rice for Hostels run by ST/SC Department for benefits of this section of the society.

SCHOOL EDUCATION

The Commission is concerned to learn from the report of the Special Rapporteur that a large number of primary schools are having a single teacher and/or being run from a single room. This is not a satisfactory situation at all. This glaring deficiency would actually affect the improvement of educational facilities and needs to be addressed with all seriousness by the State Government .

The Commission recommends a thorough review of the educational infrastructure and position of teachers especially in predominantly tribal pockets of these districts and for taking urgent remedial steps, so that the laudable efforts of improving educational facilities are not frustrated.

MONITORING

The Commission is pleased to notice that the report of the Special Rapporteur presents a fairly satisfactory picture of the execution of the Long Term Action Plan under various heads which have been considered and dealt with in the preceding paragraphs and also earlier proceedings of the Commission.

The Commission also notes with satisfaction that an officer of the status of Chief Secretary has been posted as Chief Administrator, KBK with HQs at Koraput. The Commission notices that the system of monitoring of the RLTAP made through the State Level Committee headed by the Chief Minister; the Project Level Committee headed by the Chief Secretary and the District Level Committees headed by Revenue Divisional Commissioners, supplemented by the Management Information System (MIS) broadly accords with the recommendations made by the Commission in its proceedings dated 17 January,. 2003 which were broadly based on the suggestions made by Shri Sanjay Parikh, Counsel for the petitioners. However, it is noticed that one of the most vital components of the comprehensive monitoring mechanism suggested by Shri Parikh which provides for people's participation in the endeavours through a system of public hearing has not yet been introduced. The report of the Special Rapporteur reveals that the suggestions of Shri Parikh regarding people's participation through public hearings had also been endorsed by Shri M.V. Rajasekharan, Minister of State for Planning, independently. The latest Action Taken Report filed by the State Government states that Chief Administrator, KBK and the Deputy Chief Administrator, KBK hold public hearings in the KBK districts and hear grievances of local people. The Commission was informed that it had been decided to disclose the key parameters of relevant projects including funds utilization, targets fixed and achieved at prominent places for public scrutiny. That indeed would be a good step. The Commission is of the view that a monitoring mechanism needs to be institutionalized and strengthened and people's active participation through awareness generation should be encouraged.

During the final hearing in the Commission on 18 July 2006, Shri Sanjay Parikh, learned Counsel for the petitioner, had made oral submissions. As already noticed, he had also sought permission to file detailed written submissions after taking note of the Action Taken Compliance Report of the State Government and the report of the Special Rapporteur. He has since filed the written submissions on 1 August. 2006, detailing the problems of KBK region and made certain suggestions regarding the monitoring process to be followed for implementation of the various schemes by the State/Central Government, keeping in view the recommendations made from time to time by the Commission during the hearing of this case. Learned counsel has pointed out that after identification of the problems and adoption of appropriate measures to find solutions, the real challenge now is about the monitoring of implementation of the relief and development schemes, particularly in areas which are crucial to the ultimate empowerment of the people. According to him, even after nearly a decade of vigorous monitoring by the Commission, there are still many areas which require proper planning and time-bound solutions and actions. He has therefore requested that the Commission may recommend the continuance of the RLTAP which has proved its usefulness in tackling the problems of drought, deprivation and extreme poverty of the people of this region for the time being. He has requested the Commission to issue directions for an early finalization of the latest BPL survey to enable all such families to be covered thereby to derive full benefits of the poverty alleviation programmes. Shri Sanjay Parikh has, in his submission, pointed out some important components of various welfare schemes, such as drinking water supply, primary health-care, social security pension etc which require constant attention of the State Govt and the monitoring authorities. He has suggested a system of **a quarterly monitoring method** for the implementation of RLTAP and a **monthly special monitoring mechanism** in the three sensitive areas, namely Drinking Water, Primary Health and Emergency Feeding on a regular and continuing basis.

The Commission has given its careful consideration to the submissions made by Shri Sanjay Parikh as well as the report submitted by Shri Chaman Lal and is of the view that the monitoring mechanism suggested by Shri Parikh deserves to be seriously considered and introduced as it would ensure transparency, public participation, and an inbuilt check for fixing accountability. Shri Sanjay Parikh had expressed his keenness to visit KBK districts at his own expense to see the on-going relief and development work and see how the process of people's empowerment can be expedited. The Commission finds his suggestion in that behalf deserves consideration and directs that a copy of the written submissions and note filed by Shri Sanjay Parikh be forwarded to the State Government, which may find it useful in formulating a comprehensive monitoring mechanism for the RLTAP and since he wishes to visit KBK districts at his own expense, the State Government may assist him to properly conduct the survey by its cooperative attitude.

REVISED LONG TERM ACTION PLAN (RLTAP)

Poverty by itself is the greatest violator of human rights. it poses a grave threat not only to the dignity of human beings but also the enjoyment of their most precious right — right to life. It is a fundamental right of the citizens to be free from hunger. The prevalence of extreme poverty and hunger is unconscionable in this day and age, for not only does it militate against respect for human rights, but it also undermines the prospects of peace and harmony within a State. Violation of human rights anywhere is a threat to human rights everywhere. All efforts are therefore required to be made to eradicate it and the sooner the better. The Special Rapporteur has, in his report, pointed out certain peculiar aspects of poverty in the KBK region in terms of its depth and severity which distinguishes it from prevalence of poverty in other parts of the country and calls for special strategies to be adopted and concerted action like the RLTAP to be vigorously followed. We are sure the State Government would give proper attention to it.

In his submissions before the Commission, during the final hearing, the Chief Administrator, KBK submitted that during the last three years, because of cent percent utilization of the funds provided, significant achievements had been made in all sectors covered by the RLTAP, particularly in the areas of Drinking Water, Irrigation, Welfare of SC/ST and Rural Development. He however, fairly conceded that there was much more that still remained to be done in the field of Social Security, Primary Health Care, Soil Conservation and Afforestation and has assured the Commission that the State would work with proper zeal to undo the shortcomings. The Chief Administrator, KBK, referred to the utility of RLTAP and pleaded for its continuation. The Special Secretary, Planning and Coordination, Orissa, explained the significance of RLTAP with its broad strategies aiming at (i) building rural productive infrastructure, (ii) Developing programmes for income generation on a sustainable basis (iii) Mobilising and energizing the rural poor, and (iv) Restructuring and energizing the social security system.

It would, thus, be seen that the RLTAP has proved to be highly useful to deal with the situation which was prevailing in the KBK region and came up for consideration of the Hon'ble Supreme Court and this Commission. **Considering the crucial role of the RLTAP in achieving the ultimate objectives of drought proofing, poverty alleviation and development saturation to improving the quality of life of the people in KBK districts, the Commission recommends to the Planning Commission, Government of India, for further extension of the RLTAP beyond March 2007. It also recommends**

execution of all its projects under a system of surveillance and monitoring described above and detailed in the report of the Special Rapporteur and written submissions of Shri Sanjay Parikh.

This now brings the role of the Commission to its conclusion in so far as the case is concerned. The Commission records with appreciation that the State Government took various suggestions made by the Commission in their correct spirit and it is hoped that various recommendations and suggestions made in the preceding paragraphs would receive encouraging action both by the State Government as well as the Government of India.

Before parting with the case, the Commission would like, once again, to put on record its deep appreciation for the able and constructive contributions it has received throughout the hearing of the matter from the learned counsels Shri Sanjay Parikh (for the petitioners), Jayant Das and Raj Kumar Mehta (for the State Government of Orissa) and Ajay Kumar Vali (for the Union of India). Each one of them projected the case in a very fair and objective manner and made useful suggestions from time to time, which helped the Commission to make its recommendations during the preceding hearings. The State Government has also been of great assistance to the Commission in carrying out the tasks assigned to it by the Commission, which was being monitored by the Commission on a continuing basis. The Government of India has also been very cooperative and responsive. The Commission expresses its deep sense of gratitude to Dr. Amrita Rangaswami, Director, CSAR for intellectual inputs and valued assistance she has been providing throughout the consideration of this matter by the Commission.

The able assistance offered to the Commission by its Special Rapporteur, Shri Chaman Lal, has been of tremendous value. He not only untiringly conducted a number of field visits and interacted with all concerned but also from time to time submitted very comprehensive reports. He has been making very useful suggestions to the Commission for completing its task assigned by the Hon'ble Supreme Court of India and the Commission places on record its deep appreciation for the services rendered by him.

Let a copy of this final report, which needs to be read in continuation of the earlier report made by the Commission and submitted to the

Hon'ble Supreme Court of India from time to time, be forwarded to the Registrar General of the Supreme Court of India, in compliance with the directions of the Court contained in order dated 26 July 1997 (Supra), for placing it before their Lordships.

New Delhi
30th August 2006

Appendix G

IN THE SUPREME COURT OF INDIA
CIVIL ORIGINAL JURISDICTION
WRIT PETITION (C) NO. 42 OF 1997

Indian Council of Legal Aid & Advice & Ors. ...Petitioners

Vs.

State of Orissa & Anr. ...Respondents

WITH

TC(C) Nos. 9-10/1997

ORDER

This writ petition has been filed highlighting the problems of residents of KBK districts in the State of Orissa and seeking directions to prevent starvation deaths and occurrence of famines etc.

On 28.4.1997, this Hon'ble Court noted that the National Human Rights Commissions (for short 'NHRC') was seized of the matter and recorded the submission of the learned Advocate General of State of Orissa that the State Government will implement all directions including those interim in nature, given by NHRC. In the subsequent order dated 21.7.1997, the petitioners were permitted to approach the NHRC with suggestions, for interim directions. NHRC evolved short term and long term schemes to empower the people of this region and also monitored implementation of such schemes for more than eight years. It submitted several interim reports to this Court. On 10.3.2003, this Court noted:

> It is brought to our notice that in the light of the progress made in the matter before the NHRC, the matter should continue to be considered by the NHRC itself and further orders are not required by this Court at this stage. It is ordered accordingly. The report filed so far shall, therefore, stand accepted.

Various recommendations made by the NHRC have empowered the people residing in the locality by providing them with land, irrigation facilities and opportunity to live with some dignity. The monitoring mechanism suggested by NHRC also ensured that the recommendations were implemented. Both the Union of India and the State Government cooperated well and with the joint efforts of all concerned, it is stated that a perceptible change has been brought about in the KBK area, which had earlier been termed as a problem beyond redemption.

The final report with appropriate recommendations has been given by NHRC on 30.8.2006. These recommendations will go a long way in improving the living conditions of the KBK region. The recommendations in the final report of NHRC have been accepted by the State Government. The State Government has also agreed for an effective monitoring mechanism suggested by NHRC to ensure that the suggestions made by the NHRC are implemented properly and continuously.

In the circumstances, we are of the view that no further directions are required in this petition and the connected transferred case. The writ petition and transferred case are disposed of accordingly recording our appreciation for the efforts taken by the petitioners.

If there is any difficulty, the petitioners would be at liberty to approach this Court.

22.1.2008

List of Abbreviations

AOFFP	Area Oriented Fuel Fodder Project
ATR	Action Taken Report
BP	Block Plantation
BPL	Below Poverty Line
CHC	Community Health Center
CSB	Corned Soya Blend
DLC	District Level Committee
DPAP	Drought Prone Areas Programme
DRDA	District Rural Development Agency
EAS	Employment Assurance Scheme
EFP	Emergency Feeding Programme
FCI	Food Corporation of India
GP	Gram Panchayat
IAEP	Integrated Afforestation and Eco-Development Programme
IAY	Indira Awaas Yojana
ICDS	Integrated Child Development Service
IIFM	Indian Institute of Forest Management
IIM	Indian Institute of Management
IMR	Infant Mortality Rate
ISRO	Indian Space Research Organization
IWDP	Integrated Wastelands Development Programme
JGSY	Jawahar Gram Samridhi Yojana
JRY	Jawahar Rozgar Yojna
KBK	Kalahandi Balangir Koraput

LTAP	Long Term Action Plan
MDM	Mid Day Meal
MFP	Minor Forest Produce
MHU	Mobile Health Unit
MORAE	Ministry of Rural Affairs and Employment
MMR	Maternal Mortality Ratio
MWS	Million Wells Scheme
NCAP	Non-Commutable Allocated Pension
NFBS	National Family Benefit Scheme
NFI	Nutrition Foundation of India
NOAP	National Old Age Pension
NHRC	National Human Rights Commission
NTFP	Non Timber Forest Produce
NTMFP	Non Timber Minor Forest Produce
NWDPRA	National Watershed Development Programme for Rain fed Areas
ODP	Odisha Disability Pension
PDS	Public Distribution System
PHC	Primary Health Center
PUCL	People's Union for Civil Liberties
RDF	Rehabilitation of Degraded Forests
RLTAP	Revised Long Term Action Plan
RWSS	Rural Water Supply and Sanitation
SEM	Self Employed Mechanics
SOAP	State Old Age Pension
SC	Scheduled Castes
SDGs	Sustainable Development Goals
SGRY	Sampoorna Grameen Rozgar Yojana
SGSY	Swarnajayanti Gram Swarozgar Yojana
SNP	Supplementary Nutrition Programme
SSS	Social Security Schemes

ST	Scheduled Tribes
UDHR	Universal Declaration of Human Rights
UN	United Nations
VSS	Vana Samrakshana Samithi

□□